Annie Painted Purple

Based on a true story

By

Rosemary J. McCutcheon

ISBN: 0-75966-124-3

This book is printed on acid free paper.

1stBooks - rev. 10/03/01

ACKNOWLEDGMENT

Thank you to my husband, children, grandchildren, and my very best friends who faithfully encouraged me throughout the process of writing this book.

I also want to bless Julie, who graciously edited my first book.

My prayer is that the story of **Annie** will bless all who read about her.

CHAPTER ONE

"I think I was just born," Annie mooed quietly to herself. She squinted through the fresh membrane over her deep brown eyes but could see only unidentifiable shadows.

"Yes, yes, now I remember. While I was still in the birth sac I was playing with my hoof and all of a sudden I felt myself rushing downward and I became frightened. The force, oh, the force, plummeted down, down. An unfamiliar object grasped my ear and then my head. I did not want to leave my safe home, but it was too late. My shoulders had been removed from the warmth, and I began to shiver. My back left leg was wedged, and once again I felt the unfamiliar object tugging. Ouch, I mooed, but it just kept pulling. I tried to kick, but the object held a tight grasp until my leg became free. I bawled really loud as I hit the hard ground. Then, suddenly, I felt myself totally suspended and gently placed in the warmth of loving but strange skinny hooves; nothing like I thought my Mother would feel like."

"So, all this is what Mother spoke so softly but firmly about when I was in her womb. Her voice was always so kind and gentle as she stammered and stuttered to explain how I began and what kind of calf I would be in this wonderful world. I rarely paid much attention and certainly didn't even know what a 'world' was. Just developing kept me too busy jumping and bouncing in my birth sac."

"My favorite part of development was the heart. It started out just a tiny thump and then became annoyingly loud. Vibration from the sound waves rushing through the most sensitive area of my eardrum increased the noise level of the blood as it swiftly traveled through my veins. Sometimes the perfect rhythm of the heartbeat would keep me awake, and I would tell it to be quiet! Thank goodness, it didn't listen to me or I would be dead now."

"Eventually the ingenious creation of my ears responded to the sound of each rhythmic beat pounding out the message of life, as blood pumped throughout hundreds of vessels. At times I would hear Mother coo as she listened to the beat. I bet it wasn't as loud out there."

"When my brain began to form it was incredible. It was a mass of pinkish gray tissue encased in the protective cranium. All the twists and turns of about ten billion nerve cells kept my head spinning trying to think too much. After a while I became weary just watching the intricacy and refocused on all four of my hooves. They entertained me for days at a time. Each time that I would kick really hard, I would get this scolding echo from the outside. 'Stop whatever you are doing in there,' as Mother lifted her back leg to rearrange my position."

"Oh, yes, my tongue was quite intriguing too. At first notice it was thin and didn't weigh too much, so I would try and wrap it all the way around my head. As it became thicker and heavier the challenge was delightful. I gave a big slurp one afternoon, and it went everywhere. What fun that was! I startled my Mother so bad when I shrieked with excitement, that she shook with a force that bounced me all over my sac. I was giggling so hard that I hiccuped."

"Now, one thing that really bothered me during this creation process was all the hair on my body. It was bristly and stubbly and itchy at first. I was too busy scratching, tossing, and tumbling, trying to get comfortable, to notice the rapid growth. One night right at bedtime I suddenly discovered a softness that I hadn't noticed before. My coat completely covered me. I tried to check the color but couldn't quite tell because of the darkness."

"Whew, my stomach was weird looking; it had four compartments with an opening at the end connecting to a huge squiggly rope. I think this was my large intestine. When my stomach was finished making itself, it just plopped right in place and gurgled when I would suck on my hoof."

"I think my eyes were always there because they would move back and forth in constant motion to oversee my organs, muscles, and bones come together."

Annie jolted back to the thought of her birthing process. She called out to Mother to tell her she was sorry she didn't listen. "Tell me, oh tell me, am I a heifer or a bull! Mother, what happens next? Mother, where are you? Can anyone hear me out here in this world?" Annie called. But there was no response, only silence.

Annie began coughing, sputtering, and mooing louder. Something kept wiping her face and sticking a big tool in her mouth to clear a path to help her breath. She heard noises but recognized none of them. Her moo became stronger and louder. She bawled and bawled, sensing something wasn't normal. Annie's eyes began clearing a little. She could see a bit more now, but everything still remained fuzzy.

"I think I see Mother. No, that couldn't be, but it must be. She is talking gently to me just like Mother did when I was inside, but her voice is not the same. Why isn't she mooing like she used to? It seems strange somehow. I guess I really didn't know what she would look like or how her hooves would feel around me for the first time. The same love is there but...oh, I am so confused. Can someone please tell me what is going on?" Annie cried.

CHAPTER TWO

Annie's mother, Maggie, was a beautiful Hereford from the J Bar J Ranch. The very unusual markings on her deep brown-colored hide, her one ear snow white with a hint of brown just around the tip, a white hoof on her hind leg, and two perfectly shaped butterflies, in flight, on her rear flank had won her a blue ribbon at the County 4H Fair last year. But as a young calf, Maggie had been injured when a tractor driven by Kianta struck her while she romped and played in the field.

Kianta was a fun-loving, bright, college student from Madagascar, a small island off the coast of Africa, where the population is divided into about twenty ethnic groups. Kianta was part of the Mahafaly group, which means the Joyful People. Kianta spoke fluent English and used his native language of Malagasy only when he was frustrated or playing practical jokes on other students.

Kianta had sparkling, deep brown eyes that matched his beautiful skin. Each time he laughed, the corners of his eyes would wrinkle, and his long, silky eyelashes would curl upward nearly touching the eyebrows. Kianta was lean and tall in stature; he wore his faded jeans un-belted and slightly below the waist, and he always wore a bright colored tee shirt that hugged his slender torso. Kianta was single, but he made it quite clear he was uninterested in serious dating until he finished his education.

The infant mortality rate was very high in the rural areas of Madagascar, and the village had little knowledge of farming skills. Kianta decided to come to the United States to study pediatric medicine. He also wanted to learn as much about agriculture as possible, so he decided to apply for positions that would familiarize him with farm life. Jack and Jan, of J Bar J Ranch, were searching for reliable workers, and Kianta was chosen from several applicants to work in the fields harvesting hay for the summer. Kianta, not yet an experienced farmer, loved driving anything, and Jack was confident that Kianta would be able to handle a tractor in the field.

Kianta and Maggie met quite by accident one rainy afternoon. Kianta was instructed to go to the pottery barn to begin removing some dead tree trunks by the back of the building. They were full of thousands of termites, and Jan didn't want the termites to spread to the wood on the barn. Kianta was trying desperately to avoid the swarms as he tugged on the rotten wood. The surrounding grass was very slippery. One tug. Another tug. Then another. Finally, a huge piece of wood broke free and sent him reeling backward, tumbling down the small hill.

Splat, he went, right into a pile of Maggie's warm, cow manure. Disgusted, he began flailing his arms and speaking Malagasy as he tried to free himself. The more he tried getting up, the more he slipped. He was furiously trying to keep the manure away from his head, especially his mouth!

Maggie was standing nearby observing the whole scene, trying to muffle the laughter that was bubbling up inside of her. But watching Kianta slip one way and slide another only increased the bubbling. Maggie absolutely couldn't hold it back any longer. Her tummy bounced on the soft dirt when she fell to the ground laughing, "Moo-ha-ha. Moo-ha-ha."

Kianta turned toward the noise, certain that he heard a calf laughing.

Maggie thrust her hoof into portions of smeared manure and playfully flicked it on Kianta. The scowl on his face revealed his displeasure as he tried to reach out to kick Maggie. Kianta slipped and fell backward again. Maggie, still laughing, began to crawl on her knees toward Kianta. Kianta watched for a moment—not sure whether to try and get up, or just sit and stare at this strange American calf coming toward him.

Maggie, still on her knees, stopped one foot from Kianta, grinned big enough so you could see the space between her two front teeth, and stared at him eyeball to eyeball.

Kianta, looking for any weapon he may use to distract this calf, found only a patch of tough Johnson grass surrounding him. He reached out, yanked a blade of grass from the field, and began waving it frantically at Maggie. "Shoo, shoo. Now go away, you strange calf," he cried.

Instead of scaring Maggie, the grass tickled her as it brushed across her nose. She lifted her head high in the air. "Ah, ah, ah-choo," Maggie sneezed. It was the biggest, grossest sneeze ever. Kianta screamed as he began wiping slobber and Maggie's nasal mucous from his face.

Kianta grabbed more grass and wiped his face enough to clear one eye. With the other eye still shut, he squinted to see where Maggie was. Crawling on all fours, Kianta rapidly charged toward Maggie stopping just short of ramming her. He glared with fury right into her face.

Unsure what Kianta might do, Maggie scrambled to get to her feet. Some of the warm cow manure had dribbled off Kianta where Maggie lay, causing her to slip and slide as she tried scooting on her knees to a drier area. Kianta grabbed both of Maggie's back legs. Maggie, pulling Kianta on his belly across the wet manure, struggled to free herself. But the taut muscles on Kianta's forearms revealed his strength. Maggie realized she may have to reverse her method, so she decided to relax just enough to catch Kianta off guard. She went limp, and he loosened his grip. Maggie quickly turned, lunged forward, opened her mouth wide, and with one big swipe, licked Kianta from his forehead down to his chin. Kianta let out a yelp of disgust in Malagasy. Maggie tried to run again, but Kianta was too quick for her this time. He grabbed her by the tail and pulled her down to the ground.

Trying to escape the slimy manure, both Kianta and Maggie flopped around like two fish out of water. The whole situation had become quite amusing. Kianta became very giddy. Curling his lips upward and thrusting his head backward, he began mooing and mocking Maggie.

Now, Maggie was the one staring at Kianta, thinking he was one very strange human.

Still mooing, Kianta turned and spotted a hose hanging on a rusty nail by the barn. He began dragging himself in that direction so he could get close enough to reach the nozzle. The water valve turned easily, and Kianta's fury from a few moments ago turned playful. He placed his thumb over the tip of the hose and spewed water all over Maggie, then himself. The odor was intoxicating as the manure washed down the hillside. Kianta's face was streaked with stains of green grass as tears of laughter ran down his cheeks. Maggie, dripping wet, joined in the laughter.

Sloshing around in a puddle that had formed under their feet, Kianta and Maggie managed to get themselves almost clean again. Maggie kept rubbing against Kianta to try and find a dry spot because she didn't like water on her face. Kianta playfully pushed Maggie away. Kianta ran.

Maggie chased him. Both Kianta and Maggie were quite unsightly from the manure fiasco. They laughed and poked fun at one another.

Suddenly, Kianta stopped laughing. He remembered how he had gotten in this predicament. "See what trouble you got me into calf. The termites probably have eaten the whole barn by now," Kianta scolded as he turned to hang the hose back on the nail and return to his assigned task.

Maggie followed Kianta everywhere he went—to the pottery barn, to the tree stumps, to get the axe and shovel from the work shed, to get a drink. Maggie always followed so close that Kianta's feet would become entangled with her hooves. Trying to untangle his two feet from Maggie's four hooves appeared quite ungraceful, as a ballerina might look trying to dance to rock music. Although Maggie was always underfoot, Kianta approvingly patted her smooth body from her head to her flank as he continued working.

"Well, calf, the sun seems to be whispering good night while it slips away to make room for the moon. To me that means it is time to go get some J Bar J grub," Kianta said hungrily. Who feeds you?" Kianta asked Maggie, as he rubbed his eyes and propped the old, splintered, axe beside the half-eaten tree stump. Maggie responded by turning toward the hay bale in the pasture. "I'll see you tomorrow calf," Kianta called.

"My name is not calf. Jack will tell you that it is Maggie," she mumbled, curling her forehead into a frown as she meandered down the hill.

Maggie loved Kianta and continued to follow him everywhere. Kianta's one very strict rule for Maggie was that he forbid her to enter the fields where he worked during harvest. This rule especially applied when the farm machinery was in motion. At harvest time the activity in the hay fields increased and lasted from the time the sun first appeared in the sky until dusk each evening. Maggie felt deserted because Kianta worked so many long hours. She only wanted to play with her dearest friend, and one day she decided that it would not hurt anyone to disobey this foolish rule just once. Without giving much thought to the consequences, Maggie finagled a way to get through the fence that separated her from the pasture. By using both front hooves, she dug a rut under the electric fence. Then, she was able to lay close to the ground and scoot her entire body through to the forbidden pasture. Careful not to touch any part of the electric power running through the fence, Maggie made sure her back end was totally free before she climbed to the flat section of the pasture to set out and find Kianta.

The summer rains were expected soon and Jack knew that time was of the essence to get all the hay in before the rain began. He, Kianta, and Jan diligently worked to harvest as many bales of hay as possible. Evening was rapidly approaching. Kianta was relying on the tractor headlights to light the path as he carelessly sped through each row of hay. Following the sound of the music and recognizing his voice as he sang, Maggie knew that Kianta was near. Maggie began running so fast that her ears were pinned back by the wind. The speed in which she ran prevented her from stopping in time to avoid the path of the tractor. Singing loudly, along with the music on the tractor radio, he did not hear Maggie bellow as the rear tractor wheel caught her in the left hip. The force of the tractor sent her tumbling end to end, landing face down one hundred feet away. Kianta felt the heavy thud, but he thought it was one of the many rocks protruding out of the ground, so he continued mowing.

Jan looked up in time to see the shadow of the tractor as it was speeding toward Maggie, but she could not get Kianta's attention to alert him before the rear wheel hit her.

Jan grabbed her flashlight, waved it in the air to forewarn Jack of trouble, and bolted over to rescue Maggie. Maggie was shaken but didn't seem to be in any immediate danger. Jack helped Jan load Maggie onto the wagon. Jan jumped into the wagon with Maggie. Jack climbed into the tractor seat and hurriedly sped to the barn. As Jack drove, Jan looked at every inch of Maggie to assess the damage, but she found no major injury. After making Maggie comfortable in the warm stall, Jan headed back out to the field to find Kianta.

Seeing the commotion, Kianta turned off his radio and sped toward the barn. Jan explained what had happened. The pained look on Kianta's face revealed the emotions he felt at this moment. He was not only crushed to know he had brought harm to Maggie but was disturbed at his carelessness while driving the tractor. He hurried over to where Maggie lay and plopped down beside her. Lifting her head gently onto his lap, he began crying and tenderly speaking in Malagasy. Maggie mooed ever so softly, "Kianta, my friend, I know that you didn't mean to hurt me. Besides, I was the one who was wrong for disobeying the safe rule you made to protect me. I only wanted to play."

Although Kianta nurtured Maggie back to health throughout the rest of the summer, she was still left with a slight limp from the injured hip.

It soon became time for Kianta to return to fall classes at college. The van was loaded with noisy students when it pulled into the driveway to pick up Kianta.

One more time Kianta stopped to look around J Bar J Ranch. He wanted the fun he had and the lessons he learned etched forever in his memory. Stepping from the porch onto the rock driveway, he took a very deep breath of the fresh air and said a quiet prayer of thanks.

Before getting into the van, he dropped his half zipped suitcase on the steps and ran over to give hugs to Jack, Jan, and Maggie.

A huge tear flowed over Maggie's bottom eyelid and rushed down her cheek when Kianta hugged her tightly. Kianta removed his already stained handkerchief from his back pocket and gently wiped away the tear. "Maggie, don't cry. I will stay in touch-by e-mail," Kianta joked.

Then, Maggie couldn't be sad anymore. Once again her wide grin showed the gap between her teeth. She watched Kianta grab his suitcase and squeeze between two other students in the back seat of the van. Kianta reached his long arm across one of the students to wave a last good-bye. Jan waved both arms and threw kisses as the van drove out of sight.

CHAPTER THREE

The limp in Maggie's back leg never seemed very threatening or noticeable, until she became pregnant with Annie. Throughout her pregnancy Maggie was very moody and didn't eat well. Maggie limped more than usual and expressed her discomfort by the tone of her continual mooing. As time grew near to the birth of her calf, she was listless and stayed close to familiar surroundings. Jan sensed that Maggie was in serious trouble.

Jan monitored Maggie's condition faithfully, and each day Jan would hitch the small wagon to her truck to carry the tub full of fresh water for Maggie to drink. Even then, Maggie drank little and would eat nothing.

The time to deliver approached. Maggie managed to lift herself up so she could go to a safe place to have her calf. The heavy weight of carrying a full-term calf to another location became more than her injured body could bear.

Sadly, Maggie died during Annie's birth.

A newborn calf cannot survive if it doesn't drink the mother's colostrum within twenty-four hours of birth. The colostrum provides not only strength but also immunity to all diseases for about four months. Maggie had to be milked immediately.

"Mmm. That tastes good!" mooed Annie as the nipple of the bottle was placed in her mouth. "But, Mother told me there would be several nipples to choose from." As Annie turned to look for more she lost her grip on the nipple and the milk spewed out of her mouth, down her chin, and all over her leg. When she found the nipple again Annie thought, "This must be my Mother feeding me. It is the same voice I heard when was I born. What a funny looking cow. Why does she walk on just two legs? I can't do that yet. Maybe I will be able to later. Her coat is stubby like mine used to be, and it is not all the same color," Annie studied.

Annie bobbed her head in all directions to compare her coat. "I heard Mother say that I am tan and have a beautiful, black birthmark with white dots, on hind my leg. She said I have huge brown eyes too. I also remember Mother telling me about different colors of calves when she talked to me in the sac. I think your appearance has something to do with who your mother and father are."

"This must be the barn where I will live. It is big, dark, old, and a little scary. You can feel it swaying and creaking when the wind blows just like Mother said it would. She talked about the red roof being all faded and full of holes, especially on the North side where the rain drizzles in. She said to find a stall on the South side with plenty of clean, fresh straw to keep me warm and dry," Annie remembered.

"I can't wait until I can get up to run and play with the other calves. Mother told me I would have lots of friends to romp with in the pasture. She explained how each newborn calf must stay near it's mother for a short time before becoming too venturesome. Predators were always lurking to find food and prey upon the young and injured. I asked her what a predator was. She told me that hungry animals are always creeping about looking for food and usually attacking small or injured animals that were left unattended. Well now, that got my attention. I decided I would never leave her side until I died."

"Mother, where are you? You said I should stay close. I can't see you. Will you come nearer? Mother, can you hear me? Moo, moo, moo. I am frightened. Where are all my friends? I think I am in this big old barn by myself." Annie mooed louder!

Suddenly, a noise startled Annie. The door hinges squeaked as the door opened slightly.

Annie stuck her wet nose through the wooden fence. Her eyes became wide with surprise as she caught a glimpse of the outside. "I see the pasture, I see the pasture. I just know that is the pasture—there is green grass and it is so big, just like Mother said." Annie squealed with delight.

The brisk wind caused the door to open a little wider. "That must be the way to the pasture." Annie squealed again.

Annie grunted and groaned as she tried to get up and go look for her mother. Annie kicked and pushed to stand, but she became tired and toppled over. Another try and then another. But Annie's muscle tone had not developed well enough to let her completely stand on her own without wobbling. "I'll never get out of her," Annie thought. The wind caught the door once again and slammed it shut with a loud bang. Annie was so startled that she began crying and cried all night long. When she finally drifted off to sleep she was immediately awakened by Rosa Rooster's early morning "Cock- a-doodle-doo."

Annie heard voices but didn't even raise her head when the door opened this time. She was too disappointed from not being able to get up earlier. But she did raise her eyes when she heard, "Annie, I am here to feed you," as Jan entered the barn. It sounded just like her Mother's voice, but she had not heard Jan call her by a name before.

Annie's moo was faint. She looked right into Jan's eyes and very softly tried to say, "Mother I thought you said that we would have so much fun when I was born. Well, I am not having any fun and I don't want to be here.

I can't even get up. Just go away and leave me alone," Annie sobbed. A big tear ran down Annie's cheek as Jan continued to try to feed her. Jan was acutely aware that Annie must eat from the bottle until she could be weaned, which usually occurred after four months. Jan was truly concerned because she knew this was a very critical time for Annie's survival.

"Annie, you must eat," Jan begged. Again, no response. Jan stroked Annie's head and assured her everything would be all right. Her soft-spoken voice did comfort Annie, but the ache in her heart was too great to tell Jan that she just couldn't eat right now. Maybe tomorrow.

Jan's shoulders slumped as she picked up the bottle and began walking toward the door. Annie's eyes followed Jan and she tried to moo, "Come back, Mother, don't leave me alone to die in this dark, smelly place. Please hold me. I am cold." Then Annie drifted off to sleep once again.

As Jan approached the house, Sam, the family hound, began whining because he knew something was wrong. He licked her hand and playfully tugged at the bottle. He tumbled and rolled in the grass to try and cheer her up. He ran around in circles grabbing his tail. He pushed the ball to her feet so she could kick it back. Finally, his tactics worked. Jan began to laugh. Then Jan's determination to save Annie overcame her pity as she remembered how she had saved Sam when he was just a puppy.

Sam's mother was Zuzzah. Zuzzah was an old family name that had been passed down for generations to all the female dogs since the 1800s. Well, maybe that was a little exaggerated, but Sam remained happy that he was a male so he didn't have to carry on that name. Zuzzah died from gunshot wounds. She was in the woods chasing rabbits when Pop Shishak from the hog farm up on the hill shot at the rabbit. But he wasn't wearing his glasses and he missed, hitting Zuzzah instead.

Jan did feel like she was Annie's mother; in fact, she would have to be her mother if she wanted Annie to live! Jan straightened her shoulders, grabbed the bottle, ran down the hill, charged back into the barn, and firmly told Annie to wake up because she was going to eat and she was going to eat right now.

Weakly, Annie said, "Thank you, Mother, for coming back. I really do want to live." Jan patiently held the bottle as Annie began sucking the powdered milk replacement substitute.

"My, my, Annie you are quite an amazing, little heifer. We want to put a tag in your ear quickly so everyone will know you belong to our J Bar J Ranch," Jan said.

Annie perked up when she heard the word heifer. "Now I know that I am a girl, and Mother named me Annie. I wonder who I am named after and why she thinks I am amazing?" Annie quizzically thought.

"One more thing Annie, all the other calves had their horns removed, so you must too. The process is done with an electric heated dehorning tool, and as a rule it is painless. At one time when cattle ran wild, horns were necessary for self-preservation. But now in a tame herd calves with horns create bruises on others and tend to become bullies in the pasture. Some calves do keep their horns, however, when they are raised to perform in rodeos for bulldogging or team roping. We certainly don't want a pretty little calf like you in a rodeo or becoming a girl bully, do we, Annie?" Jan gently explained as she patted Annie's nubby horns.

Annie inhaled real big and let out a long sigh. She decided she would deal with this matter later.

Every day Jan worked from early morning to late evening with Annie to get her to stand steadily on her own. She probed and prodded, pushed and shoved, tugged and pulled. Each day Annie became a little stronger, but she remained quite thin.

Annie was four months old now. Once again the alarm went off, Jan jumped out of bed, grabbed a quick cup of coffee, and hurried down to the barn. Jan just knew this was the day that Annie was going to make it. Jan tried to quiet the squeaky door as she opened it so she wouldn't awaken Annie. At the same time Annie had pushed her way outside the stall wanting to surprise Jan. She wobbled toward the door to greet Jan and let out a loud—mouthed moo, startling Jan so bad that she fell in the door and caught Annie around the neck as they both tumbled to the dirt floor.

After recovering from the laughter, Jan told Annie she had to run back up to the house for the new rope because she felt it was safe to lead her outside the barn to see the green pasture and the other cows today. It was also time for Annie to eat other food besides milk. She needed grain and grass to munch on. Her coat was dull and had become sparsely thin and would need to be fully restored to survive the winter months.

CHAPTER FOUR

"What are you doing in here?" Annie sternly asked. A skunk had wandered in from the woods and was looking for a place to have her babies.

"Don't bother me right now, okay. I don't even feel like spraying you because I am in pain. Quit your gawking and help me build a bed for my babies," replied Stinky, which was the name Jan had given her. "I hang out in this old barn once in a while along with the other adopted animals: Rosa the rooster, Constant the cat, Ruthie the rabbit, and Phyl the filly. Jack and Jan of the J Bar J Ranch are always taking in stray animals," Stinky bragged. "Have you met Jack and Jan yet?" asked Stinky. "They are really cool because they just let you come and go as you please. Of course, that is how I got in trouble having these babies," Stinky mumbled. "Jack is the big, tall, lanky one with the mustache and glasses. He is the boss. Jan is the skinny one who always rides the tractor and tries to act like the boss," Stinky chided.

Thank goodness Annie didn't hear the part about stray animals as she was gathering straw for Stinky. It was too soon for Annie to understand about Jack and Jan. At the moment, she was wondering only how Stinky could talk so much if she was in pain like she said. "Hey, you could help you know. I am not the one having babies," Annie jokingly mused.

At that moment, Annie knew that Stinky was going to be a very good friend.

"Annie, it is time; come on out," Jan called.

"Oh, no, don't tell her I am having babies again," Stinky begged. Annie jingled the bell around her neck to let Jan know she was coming so she would not come in and find Stinky.

"Please don't tell the other animals either," Stinky yelled as Annie meandered to the door.

"Mother, I am scared. Do I have to do this today?" inquired Annie. Jan carefully led Annie through the gate, over the little bridge, and up the hill to the big pasture. As they topped the hill Annie jerked to a halt. "I am not ready for this!" Annie screamed as she ran behind Jan. She tried to turn around and run back, but Jan had a tight grip on the rope around her neck.

"Annie meet your cousins," Jan proudly proclaimed, pointing to the other cows grazing in the field. She waved her arm high in the air, motioning for Jack. Jack came running and nearly knocked Annie down as he gave her a bear hug and planted a big kiss right on her wet nose.

"Well, what do you think girl?" Jack asked.

Annie stood silently in shock. She wasn't sure of anything at this point. Annie had so many questions. Why did her Mother look so different? Why were the other calves roaming about in the pasture while she had to stay in the barn?

After what seemed like an eternity, Annie nervously peeped out from behind Jan. As Jan led reluctant Annie further out in the pasture she began introducing her to each relative as she went. "Annie meet your aunt Francy," Jan announced. "Francy has been around for a long time and is so kind and gentle," Jan said as she stroked Francy's beautiful black coat.

Jan no sooner made that statement when Francy raised her head and looked at Annie with disgust. "What are you doing out here kid? You sure are strange looking, and we don't like you. Anyway, you are an orphan and nobody wants you. So scram!" Francy remarked harshly.

"So much for kind and gentle," Annie thought. "What is an orphan?" Annie quizzed.

"You will find out soon enough; now scram," Francy said as she turned away to continue munching on the green grass.

Annie turned and nudged Jan with her nose. "Mother, what is an orphan?" Jan did not answer. Jan pulled Annie to the left as Annie tugged to go right. Annie had curiously eyed a large clump of trees on the other side of the pasture. She had seen movement and wanted to investigate.

Jan realized where she was trying to go and kindly said, "Annie, I don't think you are ready to go in that direction. Thunder usually hangs out there."

"Thunder, who is Thunder?" Annie thought as she tugged to the right again.

Jan was more stern now. "You don't understand, Annie. Thunder is a 1,200-pound bull that is very smart and very fast. His powerful horns could tear both of us apart before we could even yell, 'Jezreel.' That is a secret code that Jack and I use when we are in trouble. Believe me, Annie, when the time is right he will saunter out to find himself a girlfriend and you will see him," Jan added.

Jan continued leading Annie around the perimeter of the pasture. Annie was noticeably ignored by the other cows. As Annie and Jan slowly walked along the fence row Jan stooped down to observe a frayed section in the fence. She laid Annie's rope down for a moment to mentally pinpoint the exact location. Jack would have to come and repair it.

Annie quickly took advantage of being momentarily free and quietly stepped back about twenty paces. She lowered her head to eat like the rest of the cows but raised her eyebrows so she could see if anyone was looking. "This is my first time to eat like this, and it is not easy. My tongue gets wrapped around my eye teeth every time I get a strand of grass," Annie mumbled to herself.

"Hey, you. Slurp, slurp, slurp," Arizona and Bandit giggled in unison as they mocked Annie. "Look at her licking the grass. She has a dirty nose too." They both dropped to the ground, giggling hysterically.

"I was just testing to see if I liked it," Annie said as she lifted her back leg and planted a swift kick in Bandit's rear flank.

"Ouch," Bandit mooed real loud as he tumbled halfway down the hill.

Jan heard the commotion and came running to grab Annie's rope. "Oh, I see you have met the troublesome twins," Jan replied. "Arizona is the one with the faint shape of a cactus right above her nose, and Bandit is the one that tries to steal the grain from the other calves, thus their names," Jan announced.

"I was wondering why they had such dumb names," Annie said sarcastically as she turned her back side to them.

Arizona and Bandit privately discussed Annie as she was led away. "I think I like the girl," Bandit whispered. "She sure wasn't afraid of me, and that was a powerful kick. Wonder why Mother doesn't want us to associate with an orphan? She looks like us: four legs and four hooves, two ears, wet nose, and a tail the same length as ours. She's a little skinnier maybe, but I just don't see any difference. A calf is a calf," Bandit speculated.

"Well, I am with you," agreed Arizona

"Mother, is there any hope for me out here in this colossal, obtuse place?" Annie whined dramatically.

On and on they strolled. None of the cows wanted anything to do with Annie. They sneered and turned their heads unacceptably as she approached. Annie stopped only once to watch a baby calf suckle her mother. In her heart she knew something was missing. "Where can I find answers for this ache in my heart? Maybe Stinky will know," Annie muttered.

"Come on Annie. I think you have had enough today. We will come back tomorrow and take a walk over by the pond," Jan said. Annie didn't resist this time. She was discouraged and ready to go to the barn. Anyway, she wanted to see if the babies had arrived yet. Annie felt sure that Stinky would be waiting to hear about her day in the pasture.

CHAPTER FIVE

"Stinky, are you in here?" Annie called softly. "Hello, can you hear me?" Annie called a little louder.

"Okay, okay, I hear you. Over here on the South side by the wagon. I am slightly to the left of the broken wheel, and until you came in I was resting peacefully with the babies," Stinky growled.

"Babies? How many? What are they, heifers or bulls? May I see?" Annie begged.

Stinky chuckled. "They are not calves, Annie, they are baby skunks. Allow me to introduce you to my two girls, Mellie and Mitzy," Stinky proudly announced.

Annie charged over to have a look. Stinky instinctively reared up in defense, and then backed off after realizing that Annie was just excited and not going to hurt her babies. "Annie, one of your first lessons about a new mother is to realize that she will go to any measure to protect her young. You must be very respectful of this in the future. You may come closer now," Stinky kindly expressed.

Annie tucked her hoof underneath them and tired to roll them over. They whimpered a little, but didn't move. Then she asked how long it would be before they could play with her.

"Quite awhile, dear," laughed Stinky.

"Stinky, what is an orphan? That is all I heard in the pasture today! Ooh, look at the orphan. She is weird. We can't play with you because you are a stupid orphan. Your mother hates you and we do too," Annie exaggerated.

"Annie, while Mellie and Mitzy are asleep let's take a walk around the corral. I will try and explain as kindly as I can," Stinky said. "The night you were born I had just found out I was pregnant, and my appetite was raging. So, I went to raid the garden of any fresh vegetables I could find. Just as I had settled on the biggest carrot in the garden, I heard a weak moaning sound coming from behind the haystack. I cautiously crept over in the direction of the moan and found your beautiful Mother, Maggie, lying on the ground. Her eyes were very sad, and her breathing was labored. She struggled to roll her head to the side when she heard me coming and said, 'Please tell my baby calf that I loved her and that she should always be brave and never give up.' I turned my head away so she wouldn't see my tears, knowing that I must remain strong. I waddled over and snuggled against her neck and began humming gently," Stinky sniffed. "Then I heard the tractor coming at full speed. Jan jumped down and began weeping because she knew that Maggie wouldn't survive. Her instincts took over, and she knew she had a big night ahead of her if she was to save the calf. That was you, Annie. After you were safely delivered, Jan hurriedly milked your Mother so you could be fed her natural milk. Without that you could not have survived. The reason you are labeled an orphan is because your Mother died. Nature is funny that way. It is like you are an outcast to the world if you are a runt or abnormal in any way. Being an orphan is kind of like that. I really haven't figured it out yet, but that is the way it has always been," Stinky explained.

Annie was stunned. She didn't know what to say or do. Buckets of tears began rolling down her cheeks. Loud sobbing permeated the night air. Annie was sobbing so hard that Stinky felt the ground beneath her tremble.

"Cry, Annie, cry. It is good for the soul," Stinky shouted over Annie's bellowing. Lightning filled the evening sky and thunder clamored, startling Annie.

"Come on, girl. Let's run for the barn," Stinky called as the rain pelted against them.

When they were safe in the barn Stinky went to check on the babies and then tugged at the horse blanket thrown over the stall until the blanket tumbled to the ground. "Here, Annie, dry off with this. It will help you stay warm. Rub the water off me too," Stinky told Annie.

The storm subsided almost as quickly as it had approached, and the stillness in the barn was eery. Stinky was allowing Annie all the time she needed to collect her thoughts and grasp the meaning of the past few hours. After feeding the babies, Stinky nestled down under the horse blanket and drifted off into a very deep sleep.

By the wee hours of the morning Annie had created a rut in the dirt floor of the barn as she paced back and forth. Annie thought. Annie cried. Annie continued to pace. Stinky slept.

Dawn broke. Stinky was awakened by Mellie and Mitzy's hunger cry. Stinky stretched, yawned, and then bolted upright when she realized she had slept through the night. She began yelling as she nursed, "Annie, Annie. Where are you? Oh, Annie, are you dead?" Stinky desperately cried.

"No, I am not dead. I am very much alive and hungry," Annie called from the feeding trough. "After you went to sleep, I had a whole night to think about myself. Someone was with me, Stinky. I don't know how to explain it," Annie calmly replied. "The soft voice told me that my natural Mother died, but another one was provided to take care of me. That was Jan. I learned she is a human and that I was not left unattended or alone to die in the pasture.

Jan was there. At that moment, I knew everything would be alright. I will need your help and support, Stinky," Annie choked up as she talked.

"All right girl, but first, give me five." Stinky waddled over and bumped her buttocks up against Annie's leg. "Look out Ms. Francy; here Annie comes. Now, watch me. I am going to show you how it is done. Raise your head real high and get that steady look in your eye, Annie. Swing your tail back and forth with confidence. Stand erect like a real Hereford. Begin marching forward and pretend you own this farm," Stinky said as she pranced about with her black tail curled upward.

"No, no, Annie, not to that extreme. You are so stiff that you look like a wooden cow with a giraffe's neck. It works much better if you can see where you are going, and you sure can't do that if you have your head stuck so high in the air that you are looking through the holes of the roof. Relax your head a little and don't have your tail swinging so hard that it knocks the nails out of the railing as you walk by," Stinky laughed.

Annie was determined. She practiced until she nearly wore the bottoms off her hooves. The jiggle of her rear-end was a bit much, but it became a little less flaunted as she practiced.

While Annie practiced, Stinky crawled out the hole under the barn door to sneak up to the house to see if Jan was around. "Good, Jan is gone on her morning errands and won't be back for a while," Stinky sighed. "Okay, Annie, the coast is clear. Get your shiny hooves on because we are going for a stroll in the pasture," Stinky shouted as she crawled back through the hole.

"What about Jan? She warned me not to go out alone and to stay close to the barn," Annie gasped.

"Well, in the first place, you won't be alone. I am going with you. And secondly, Jan is not around," Stinky said firmly. "We don't have all day. Are you going or not?" Stinky commanded.

Annie regained her confidence, stood erect, and walked to the door. Pushing with her nose and sticking half of her face out the door, she looked around outside to make sure no one was there. "All clear, Stinky. You go first," Annie whispered.

Stinky thought they would be inconspicuous if they walked quietly along the fence row until they could reach the gate. But, Thunder spotted them and came stampeding down the hill snorting with fury. "Don't panic! He can't get through the fence without getting zapped by the electricity. Just keep on walking tall" Stinky said nervously.

Annie had other thoughts. She stopped, turned, and braced herself as she eyeballed Thunder. "You don't scare me you overpowering bag of wind," Annie bravely yelled as she stood on the opposite side of the fence. A dirt cloud surrounded Thunder as he screeched to a halt and stuck his hooves in the ground. Annie had caught him completely by surprise.

Thunder spit and sputtered through the dust with his face lowered to Annie's level. "What did you say, orphan? Don't you know that I could obliterate you with one gouge from my horns? I rule this kingdom," roared Thunder.

"Well, in the first place, my name is Annie, and secondly, yes, I know what you could do to me. And that still doesn't change a thing," Annie said with firmness.

Arizona and Bandit were hiding behind a half-eaten bale of hay watching with fear and trepidation. They both remained as quiet as two cats about to pounce on a mouse, unsure of what would happen next. "Go, Annie, punch kick the ole geezer," whispered Bandit.

Annie was about to make a profound statement. She had sensed a longing to see Thunder the day Jan told her he was a bull and hiding in the trees. She felt a strange sensation to find out more about this bull they called Thunder. Now that she had seen Thunder she recognized a mark in the bend of his right left leg. The mark was identical to the dark band around her hind leg. Both marks were distinctive because of the unusual white dots in perfect succession around the entire band. She instinctively knew that this was a birth mark that could be passed only along to another generation of the same blood line.

Annie's staunch was strong—not budging. She held her head high, just like Stinky said, and edged a little closer to the fence, careful not to touch it.

"Thunder, do you know why I am not afraid of you? Because I know that you are my father," Annie yelled at the top of her lungs, right in his big black face. Not a sound was heard throughout the pasture. Even Thunder's heavy breathing stopped. All the cows stopped chewing and let grass dangle out their mouths. The birds halted their flight mid-air. The leaves on the trees were intently listening. All the sheep in the neighbor's pasture raised their head in unison. Constant, Ruthie, Phyl, and Rosa became as motionless as statues when Annie's loud voice penetrated the muggy summer air. It seemed that all creation was waiting to see if Thunder would maul Annie to death.

Unseen, Mellie and Mitzy scurried out of the barn. They sensed their mother was in danger. Skunks are extremely strong for their size and, like thieves, can get anywhere unnoticed. Hurriedly, they dashed under the fence and let out a raucous screech like a Maccaw. At the same time they used their defense mechanism: they raised their tail and sprayed Thunder smack in the face, and then they bit him on the most tender part of his leg. Stinky was mortified and raced to their rescue. Thunder bellowed with fury and swiped his horns at the babies threatening to kill them. He caught Stinky instead and flung her one hundred feet in the air. Annie screamed, galloped as fast as a horse toward Stinky, and fell to the ground just in time for Stinky to land straddle on her head. Annie raised her eye but could see only Stinky's belly.

Annie immediately shook her off for fear her sprayer would accidentally discharge. Stinky was okay but shaken. Annie and Stinky looked at one another simultaneously, and screeched "Mellie, Mitzy." Lightning fast they were down by the fence looking for the babies and observing the steam coming from Thunder's nose as he continued beating his hooves against the ground. Mellie and Mitzy were quick to dart through Thunder's back legs. Their intelligent maneuver had saved their lives, and both were safely tucked out of sight in the wood pile behind the barn. All that could be seen were their tiny eyes glistening as they peeked out through the silky web that Samatra, the spider, had delicately spun. The three of them sat immobile watching and waiting.

Thunder launched into a stride almost as fast as the speed of light. He intimidated everything in his path as he furiously zigged and zagged his way up the hill. Through the pond he flew. His hooves didn't even touch the water. He was going so fast, probably because he was scared. Some say that pond was at least fifty feet deep with a swift vortex perpetually in motion ready to suck you under. The rumor was that no man or animal that even so much as put a toe in the murky water ever came out alive because of the phantom that lurked in the deep. Most were unsure whether the tale was true, but all the farmers loved the suspense as they would make up a story to tell the "young-uns" gathered around the campfire.

The pine trees lay over from the whirlwind as Thunder bolted through to the farthest corner of the pasture toward his hide out. As he approached his safe place of refuge Thunder barely had enough strength to maintain his dignity. Still standing erect he turned and looked around to make sure no one followed and then collapsed from exhaustion in a 1,200-pound heap. With his front legs curled under his head, he actually started bawling.

Charlie, the nosey old crow, just happened to be resting himself on the knotted fence post right above Thunder's head. "Well, as sure as my feathers are black, I think I hear Thunder squalling," Charlie cawed. "Oh, fearless king of the pasture," Charlie mocked. "Shall I fly away and tell the other animals that the pompous king is really a sniveling milksop," Charlie continued taunting.

"Just shut up you old blanched out bird brain," Thunder sniveled as he wiped his nose on the grass. "I am the king of this pasture. I am the biggest and most desirable bull around. I am the most feared of all," Thunder said with little assurance in his voice.

"Well, whatever you think. Each afternoon I make my rounds dining on the leftover grain lying around and I hear what all the other animals are talking about," Charley criticized. "Their conversations sure aren't favorable for Mr. King of the pasture. They not only fear you but hate you because of your arrogant mannerisms. Instead of roaming about the pasture warding off impending danger, you succinctly prance about with your big crooked horns stuck up in the air, swat flies with an attitude, and snort orders as you pass by," Charlie articulated. "That certainly is no way to gain respect. You first must earn it," Charlie dictated. "I suggest you lay here and think about it for a while, Mr. Thunder—less," Charlie cawed once again as he flew away.

CHAPTER SIX

Annie was very disheartened at Thunder's reaction. She thought maybe he would say a kind word to her when their relationship had been revealed. Only for a moment, she became disappointed in herself for being so impressionable. Then tapping her hoof in anticipation, she pondered her next move. Inspired by her Mother's voice that rang out in her heart, "Don't ever give up Annie," she promptly regained her courage and stepped forward speaking a challenge to the other animals.

"Okay, so you have been told that I am an orphan. A throwaway that probably would not amount to anything. Well, I am here to give you a brand new concept about my worth," Annie said optimistically. "It all hinges on what is in the heart, not on physical appearances. Look at me, all of you. I am really not so different. I eat, drink, run, play, tease, laugh, love, and cry just like you. And certainly after today you know that I am not afraid, especially when there is an electric fence between me and Thunder," Annie jested.

Phyl was the first to come to Annie. "Annie, I have made a decision that may cost me a few friends, but I can't stand by and watch a perfectly good calf destroyed just because someone said you are an orphan. After all, I have seen myself in a mirror, and I guess I am not as big and beautiful as a thoroughbred either. Does that make me not worth anything?" Phyl said bravely.

Stinky had gone over to help the girls out of the wood pile. She, Mellie, and Mitzy were already making their way to Annie, but Phyl had longer legs and just moved quicker to be the first one to show support for Annie.

Samatra scurried through the tall grass, crept up Annie's leg, and planted her body right between the eyes for a bird's eye view. Annie looked cross-eyed to see Samatra and told her to sit still and not spin webs.

Purring against Annie's leg with a dead mouse clenched between his teeth, Constant meowed, "I'm a carnivorous animal, I can see very well in the dark, and I can smell a rat a mile away Annie. As long as you will allow me to have my independence, I will help you."

Ruthie and her family, American Fuzzy Lop rabbits, hopped over beside Annie. They could help too by standing absolutely motionless when danger is near.

Rosa belted out, "Annie, I am a White Leghorn Rooster and will keep all those clucking chickens from eating your grain."

Bandit and Arizona's brave move sang out a loud message to the other cows as they trotted down and silently stood by Annie.

Slowly, one by one, the other cows made their way to the fence gathering around Bandit and Arizona's mother, Esther. All but Francy, that is.

The rest nodded for Esther to speak for them. "Annie dear, I am considered the queen of this herd, and on behalf of all of us I want to apologize. Not for calling you an orphan, because that is not important, but for ignoring you in a time of trouble. Any one of us could have fed you when you were born, but we were too high and mighty. We were afraid that you would contaminate our utters or be a bad influence for our calves. We are very grateful for the humans, Jack and Jan. They have fed us in the cold winters when grass was scarce and given us water to drink when the pond was iced over. Both were there when the twins were born to make sure that I did not encounter any danger.

The night you were born we watched from a distance and couldn't understand why they worked so hard to save your life. After all, you were a puny thing, the wrong color, and an orphan to boot. What an awakening for all of us today. None of those things matter. It is your heart, Annie. It may take a while for you to build your trust, but we want to be your friends too," Esther humbly spoke.

Francy stood afar, thoroughly annoyed by the actions of her peers. She just wasn't going to budge and lower her standards. Do you suppose Francy was going to be lonely by adopting this attitude?

Annie was clearly moved by such kind gestures. But she wasn't going to fade into a pile of pulp for them. "I want to thank all of you for your courage. This will change the course of cow history today. We all know that we must continue to follow the rules of the pasture: stay inside the fence, keep with your mother until she determines it is safe to stray a little, help others across the metal bridge to drink from the pond, don't steal other's grain (Annie looked directly at Bandit), and cow your posts when you are on duty to watch for unwanted intruders. In addition, I would like to propose two new rules: do not pre-judge puny or ugly animals and help Jack and Jan do their chores so they can enjoy their retirement. The cows broke out in a cheer that you could hear up by Pop Shishak's farm. The loud grunting of the hogs also echoed in agreement.

Thunder had observed the whole episode from the forest and was deliberating what to do. "I can't charge down by the fence because that would alarm all of them. But, if I just casually whistle and stroll toward the crowd they will suspect that I am concocting trouble." He stepped and stomped, trampled and tread. Then with a strand of straw between his lips he leaned up against the same knotted fence post that Charlie was perched on and let out a big sigh. "What is a king to do?"

"I'll tell you what to do you bulky coward," screeched Charlie as he descended onto a limb out of Thunder's reach. "Make you a pole to hold up a white cloth of surrender, king buffoon," Charlie giggled with victory.

"Out of here, you sad sack of bones, before I de-feather you," blared Thunder.

Caw, caw, caw, "Your majesty, Lummox." Again Charlie cruised to an altitude just out of Thunder's grasp.

"Scavenger. One day I am going to make mincemeat of that crow and serve him to the ant farm," Thunder exasperated.

Thunder was intensely aware that his status was in jeopardy as long as he remained hidden behind the trees. He warily pushed his nose through. Next he poked his head out with most of his horns visible, and then stood inaudible for a moment. Seemingly invisible, Thunder began navigating the rest of his 1,200 pounds in full view. It was now or never. He breathed deep and ambled forward toward the pasture. The tumble bugs rolled up in a ball and thrust themselves out of Thunder's path. The grasshoppers leaped high in the air warning the other insects to clear out of the way. But, Thunder was too quick. His hoof sank into the soft earth and uncovered the bees' nest burrowed in the middle of the field. Swarms of yellow jackets flew in formation to punish the intruder. They enveloped Thunder in a cloud and began their attack. He frantically swept his tail to ward them off. He mooed, bucked, stomped, and ran all the way to the pond, jumping in to escape their vicious stings, without thinking about the phantom of the deep. Like war planes, the organized attack was successful, and the bees flew away to once again return to their base.

Thunder was relieved, but then he realized where he was. He quickly put all four hooves in motion to escape the fearful waters.

Too late, the phantom emerged, flipping high in the air and smacking Thunder right on his buttocks. "You'd better run for your life; I am the chilling, creepy monster of the deep. I am the one who lurks in the seaweed waiting for my next victim," laughed Catacombs, the one-hundred pound catfish.

Even though his mother and father had long been caught and eaten, Catacombs had defied every fishermen since his birth twenty-five years ago. He would play games with fishermen, arching his back out of the water enough to reveal what appeared to be a "huge" shape of an unknown creature. Then he would stir the waters viciously as he descended to the deep, bubbles surfacing as he laughed all the way, and he would wait for the next fisherman to bait his hook with hope of snaring Catacombs with that tiny little worm. Catacombs thought it amusing how the fishermen would throw their poles, reel and all, into the water as they scrambled away in fright each time he would surface. There must be hundreds of poles on the bottom of the pond.

"You have got to be kidding?" Thunder exclaimed as his eyes bulged with surprise. "You are no more than fish bait, you scaleless little aquatic mammal. I ought to tear your whiskers right off your flat head," threatened Thunder.

"My, my, listen to the big mouth bull that is really just a namby-pamby coward? I think we have a lot in common Thunder—less. Neither of us deserves the acclaimed reputation we have acquired. I am certainly not a harmful creature and you for sure are not a king of any pasture," Catacombs informed Thunder.

"Well, uh, I am trying to make amends. I was on my way to tell the other animals to forgive me when those annoying bees attacked me," explained Thunder. "Now seems the appropriate time to expose the mystery of the pond creature, too, don't you think?" asked Thunder as he tried to get ashore.

"What? Uncover my secret? I have been the supreme being of the best fishing hole around for a long time. Give me a little time to swim around and analyze the consequences," Catacombs said with much consternation. He dove down to the bottom, back up, down again, and then resurfaced. Gracefully he swam as if he were vying for the Olympic gold, propelling himself five times around that pond.

Catacombs thought about the many tricks he played on all the fisherman and felt rather ashamed about the whole situation. He came to the conclusion that he was tired of being so lonely and could succeed only by telling the truth. Finally exhausted, he rolled over on his back and floated over near Thunder. "Okay, Thunder, after much thought I am ready to disclose the villain and let everyone know they have been afraid of something that really never existed. I have been one lonely catfish all these years," admitted Catacombs. "It may be easier if we do this together. You claim you were on your way to tell the other animals. Do you think you can try again?" asked Catacombs. "I will wait here, and you can ask all of them to come to the pond," yelled Catacombs as Thunder was swimming for shore.

Thunder was waterlogged but managed to pull himself up to the grassy area. He shook violently, sending sprays of water up in the tree where Charlie was perched watching and listening.

"Well, today is my day. Just as I suspected. No ogre. No king. Both of you have been completely dishonest all this time. What are you going to do about it?" squalled Charlie. "Would you like me to fly ahead and spill the beans to the other animals?" crowed Charlie.

"You miserable little flea bag," Thunder said through clenched teeth.

"Now Thunder, if you are going to set the record straight, you have to include that pile of feathers too," Catacombs called from the pond.

"Okay, but it won't be easy," Thunder conceded. "Charlie, if I absolutely have to be nice to you then you are going to be my forerunner," challenged Thunder. "Fly to the fence post closest to Annie and whisper in her ear that I would like to talk," Thunder commanded.

Away Charlie flew to fulfill his mission.

"Psst, Annie, over here," Charlie quietly cawed.

"Just what might a mischievous old crow want with an angelic calf like me," Annie asked sarcastically.

"Come closer and I will tell you," Charlie whispered. Annie cautiously loped over about a foot from the fence post. "Not close enough. I don't want anyone else to hear what I have to say," said Charlie.

"No pranks or I will personally pluck your prized feathers from your skinny little body," Annie threatened.

"I think you will be delighted, my dear," Charlie said smugly. "I have come on behalf of Thunder; he wants to talk to you and the other animals up by the pond. Are you willing to give him a chance?" asked Charlie.

"Let me think a minute, Charlie. I don't want to endanger anyone. This could very well be another trick," Annie said cautiously, evaluating the situation.

"I have a little time on my wings, so I will sit right here and wait for your answer," Charlie grinned.

Annie began her usual pacing. She was deep in concentration, eyes piercing the ground, tongue sweeping back and forth on her lips, and mouth muttering words of wisdom to herself. The other animals began gathering nearer to see what she was saying.

"Annie? I know that look. What are you contemplating?" asked Stinky. Annie did not immediately respond to Stinky. She was in deep thought, carefully orchestrating her next move.

"Everyone deserves a second chance," Annie mumbled. "But, what if I put everyone in jeopardy?" Annie questioned herself. "Thunder really tried to hurt the babies and could have possibly killed Stinky," Annie muttered angrily. Annie continued trying to justify her actions of not wanting to forgive Thunder.

Annie stomped loudly to awaken Charlie, who had fallen asleep and was hanging upside down by his claws on the fence post. The image confirmed her suspicion that Charlie was a little strange sometimes. "CHARLIE, WAKE UP!" Annie screamed. Charlie fell flat on his beak from the shrill outcry.

"Why you little crack-brain. Are you trying to kill me?" Charlie screeched as he straightened his feathers and rubbed his sore beak.

"Well, I tried to warn you, and anyway, you said you would be right here waiting when I was ready to talk," Annie firmly reminded Charlie. "I think I may have a workable plan. If Thunder's gesture of kindness is for real, he certainly will agree to my terms," Annie commented. "You go tell Mr. Thunder that he can just sleep on this and meet me in the morning at dawn. Tell him to be standing in full view by the old swing hanging on the oak tree by the pond. And, if he is late, it is all off," snorted Annie.

Charlie walked about to regain his composure after the fall, and without acknowledging Annie, he took flight, leaving a dust cloud behind, and headed for the pond.

Thunder was lying in the grass sunning himself, not quite asleep, just day dreaming about his girlfriend. Charlie landed with a thud on Thunder's hind quarter and the sting of his sharp claws brought Thunder back to grim reality. Thunder rolled over with a force that flipped Charlie to the ground right on his beak. Charlie was dazed and felt to see if his beak was still on his face. He moaned in pain as he began weaving back and forth trying to walk. "Not again," Charlie whined.

"You deserved that you little-uh, bundle of soft feathers," Thunder said as he avoided slandering Charlie.

"Shut up, you big oaf. I am the delivery crow, and both you and Annie are abusing me. I just may not give you the message that Annie sent. So, there," Charlie groaned.

"If you don't cooperate I will pluck out your unruly tongue, you small-brained scavenger. Now give me the message," Thunder snapped.

"Alright but I don't know Annie's plan. Remember, I am just the messenger. She said for me to tell you to sleep on it and meet her in the morning at dawn. She wants you to stand in full view by the old swing hanging on the oak tree by the pond. And, if you are late, it is all off." Charlie reported.

"If you are not telling me the truth I will hunt you down like a farmer does when you steal his corn," Thunder warned turning toward the pond. He must inform Catacombs.

CHAPTER SEVEN

"Annie, Annie. Where are you?" Jan called from the barn. Annie looked at Stinky and started running with all her might.

"Wait. I will go with you," Stinky called as Mellie and Mitzy followed. But Annie did not stop until she got to the barn.

"Annie, how did you get out here. I know that I latched the door before I left. I wonder if Jack was here while I was gone," Jan said baffled. Annie concealed how out of breath she was and nudged Jan playfully to distract her. "Stop, Annie. You are going to trip me. Stop I said," teased Jan. "Annie, you look kind of washed out. Did you have a bad day? You sweet thing. I bet you are hungry, aren't you girl?" Jan mused as she tickled Annie's chin.

Stinky was rolling with laughter as she watched Annie bat her eyes innocently. Jan turned to get some feed, and Annie gave Stinky an unapproving look, which made Stinky laugh even more. Then Mellie and Mitzy began giggling uncontrollably too. Jan circled to see what all the noise was about, but Stinky and the girls waddled quickly out of sight.

"Annie, I have some good news. You won't have to worry about dealing with Thunder. Jack and I have thought about selling him for a long time because he is becoming too aggressive with the rest of the herd. Lorenzo from the Megiddo Auction Barn has bought him and is scheduled to pick him up tonight. They will sell him to another farm where he will be used in a greater capacity," Jan announced.

Annie gasped so hard she tumbled backward into the pitchfork that was leaning against the stall, fell to the ground, knocked over the bucket of feed, and squashed Samatra, who had been hanging on her back leg when she ran for the barn.

The foundation shook, and straw fell from the loft covering Jan. She spit and sputtered, flailing her arms to keep the straw from getting into her mouth.

Stinky froze.

Annie mooed, "No, no, you can't do that. He is going to make it all right in the morning."

But Jan didn't understand Annie. Jan dusted herself off and ran to see if she could help Annie. "Annie, what is wrong. Are you hurt?" Jan anxiously asked.

Annie knew somehow she had to calm down so she could get rid of Jan and go warn Thunder.

Stinky told Mellie and Mitzy to stay put and intuitively ran out the hole under the door to get Charlie's attention.

Annie got up on her knees and acted as is she were looking for her feed, to divert Jan's attention. "Oh, girl, you are hungry." Jan scooped a handful of the spilled feed and offered it to Annie. Annie was practically gagging, but she camouflaged it well. Jan told Annie that she would leave and let her rest now. "I will see you in the morning," Jan called, latching the door behind her.

Annie raced to the door, peeping out between the cracks. "I must get out of here before they take Thunder," Annie cried desperately.

Ruthie hopped between Jan's legs just before the barn door was latched. Her sandy-colored fur blended so well with the hay strewn all over the floor of the barn that she was not noticed. A fresh sprig of dandelion leaves sticking out both sides of Ruthie's mouth indicated she had raided

Jan's herb garden again. Still hungry, Ruthie decided to see if Annie had any extra food. When she entered the barn, Ruthie sat up on her hind legs and sniffed the musty air. Her keen sense alerted her that Annie was troubled. Since Ruthie was out of the litter of rabbits from the Spring, she was still considered a baby. Her speech wasn't totally developed yet. Ruthie's tiny rounded mouth formed a circle as she asked, "What is 'twubbling' you, nannie? You 'wook' berry sad."

Annie looked into Ruthie's sweet, petite, furry face and could see the genuine concern. She bent her head down and playfully nudged Ruthie's white, cotton tail. Annie didn't want to concern Ruthie, so she diverted her attention away from the crisis. "Ruthie, why don't you go get some of my fresh hay to take to the other rabbits. And, make it quick so they won't be starving by the time you get back."

"Can I 'weally' have some of your 'fwesh' hay, instead of stealing it, nannie?" That will 'bwighten' my Mom up," Ruthie stammered. She spun her furry body around and hopped so fast over to the pile of freshly cut hay by Annie's stall, that she bumped right into Stinky, who was on her way out of the barn to find help for Annie.

Stinky hardly noticed Ruthie. She was on a very important mission to get help for Annie. Stinky continued toward her secret outlet at the back of the barn where she had to squeeze her body through to the outside. "Charlie, Charlie, where are you? Annie needs your help," Stinky called softly, thinking no one else would hear her.

"Charlie is no where around. I saw him fly to the highway to see if he could find supper. What do you want with him this time of day?" Francy snarled.

"You would be the last cow I would tell, you mean old heifer. Why are you even down this close to the barn anyway?" Stinky smarted off.

"Watch your manners, skunk. Maybe I am not as mean as you think. Besides, I have been observing the events of the day. I suspect Annie must be in trouble. Am I right?" Francy asked.

"Well, not exactly, but Thunder is," Stinky replied.

"I saw the genuine concern from Annie for all the animals today. That is more than I can say for myself. Annie is a natural born leader. I probably have misjudged her and the others terribly. My eyes have been opened in the last few hours watching Annie and the others come together. It made me realize that I, too, need to be a more considerate cow," Francy admitted openly. "I will assist you. Just tell me what you need," Francy assured Stinky.

At the moment Stinky had no other choice but to rely on Francy. She could get to Thunder quicker, and he would listen to one of his own kind rather than a skunk.

Stinky did not know that Francy was already aware of the arrangements Jack and Jan had made today. In fact, she had been partly responsible for the action against Thunder. Summer was coming to a close with Fall right around the corner. Francy was trying to get the last of the blackberries off the vine, and it was as if the vines were telling her to get out of their patch. She became entangled, covered from head to toe with scratches and bruises all over her body by the time she freed herself. To avoid getting in trouble for stealing blackberries, Francy immediately began scheming a plan to convince Jack that Thunder had mauled her. Throwing herself down on the ground in the pasture, she mooed loudly to get Jack's attention just as he was coming out to check on the level of water in all the troughs. As soon as Jack was close enough to see her, Francy lifted her head slightly to look in the direction of Thunder's hay bale.

Jack looked in the same direction and asked, "Did Thunder do this to you girl?"

Francy proceeded to moo as if she were in terrible pain, "Yes, that nasty, old ton of blubber did this!"

The truth all along was that Francy was jealous because she had never been able to have a baby calf. She blamed it all on Thunder and wanted to pay him back. It wasn't Thunder's fault. Francy was unable to bear a calf because she was too old when she was bred. Now, Francy felt so remorseful that she made up her mind to do at least one thing right and that would be to help Stinky find Thunder.

Annie tried desperately to get out of the barn. She summoned Mellie and Mitzy for help. Annie lowered her head for Mellie to climb on and raised her up to try to reach the latch on the barn door. Mellie was too small. Annie helped her down and turned to look for anything that she could push against the door to jar it open. Her eye caught the broken wagon. She backed up to the old broken wheels, dug her hooves in the dirt, and pushed with all her strength, but the door would not budge.

The ladder to the loft may be strong enough. Mellie and Mitzy helped Annie knock it over toward the door. That didn't work either; it just laid against the door blocking the way out. Annie was feeling helpless. She kicked and stomped, but the latch held tight.

"Mellie, what is that noise? What are all the people doing outside. Please crawl out and see. Come back quickly and give me a report," Annie begged. Annie was very restless, knowing something was amiss that may be out of her control.

Francy rapidly made her way to Thunder's hideout, but he wasn't there. Thunder had decided to sleep by the pond after he talked to Catacombs.

He was awakened by a shrill sound coming from the field as a frantic Francy was bawling for him. "Francy, is that you. I am over here by the pond. What on earth is wrong? Why are you not sleeping by your favorite hay bale?" Thunder questioned.

Francy continued her hysteria. Thunder had never seen her like this, and it was disturbing. Her adrenalin was pumping so fast she wasn't even afraid of Thunder. "Annie is trapped in the barn and needs to see you NOW! Follow me NOW," Francy demanded.

"Stinky was looking for Charlie, but he wasn't available, so I am the one that volunteered to come and get you for Annie. Thunder, I am so sorry for all the harm I have caused you. Please hurry," Francy cried.

Thunder agreed and launched his 1,200 pounds in motion past Francy. He was in full speed when he spotted the commotion down by the house. Stopping abruptly and then hiding behind a tree, he asked Francy if she knew why all the people were standing in the driveway. Francy began bawling and couldn't stop long enough to tell Thunder. She was too heartbroken.

Thunder heard his name and immediately knew that Jack and Lorenzo were not coming for a social visit. Before he could turn around Jack spotted him and coerced him to come eat the tasty grain from his hand. "I am not that stupid," Thunder thought. He bucked and took off running.

Francy was frantic and begged Jack to take her in Thunder's place. Jack looked right past her and pursued Thunder.

Thunder continued running to his hideout. He had one place that no one knew about except for nosey old Charlie, who managed to find out everything. Right behind the clump of briars at the rear of Thunder's private domain was a narrow tunnel that used to lead to an underground spring. A minor earthquake had caused it to cave in, but a small section remained and Thunder would occasionally retreat there for privacy.

"Charlie, go get Annie. Bring her around the back way. Hurry, I want to talk to her. It is only a matter of time before Jack finds me," Thunder mooed.

Charlie was high above the trees but heard Thunder's cries and flew to the barn. He worked feverishly to unlatch the door with his sore beak. Annie leaped through the opening just as he freed the latch and down went Charlie landing on his beak. "Not again," cawed Charlie.

Recovering quickly, Charlie spoke with a firmness Annie didn't recognize. "Annie, keep quiet and listen to me," Charlie said as he jumped on her back to hitch a ride. "I want you to do exactly as I say and don't call for anyone to go with us," Charlie commanded. "Get down on your knees and crawl through the tall grass behind the pottery barn where Jan keeps her kiln. I know you have never been there, but I will guide you," Charlie spoke softly so that not even Stinky could hear.

"Kiln, that is a funny word. What is a kiln?" asked Annie.

"A kiln is an oven or furnace for baking, burning, or drying bricks and pottery. Charlie explained. "Jan is an artist. She used to paint and sketch murals on her children's bedroom walls, but she recently became interested in making her own pottery. As Jan forms a ball of clay into a piece of pottery on her pottery wheel she designs each with a western motif. After she completes this process, she brings them to the pottery barn to be put into the kiln. That is how I am able to see her work when I am peering down from the tree top," Charlie continued.

"You really are a nosey old crow, aren't you, Charlie," Annie whispered as they continued their trek through the tall grass.

"You are going to have to get down real low to get under the electric fence," Charlie said as he lay flat across her back.

"Oooooouch," Charlie squelched a shriek as Annie went under the fence, but not low enough to keep his right wing from getting a jolt of electricity.

"Yikes, are you okay, Charlie?" Annie chuckled.

"You just fried my feathers you little, uh, darling." Charlie refrained from being too harsh, remembering his mission. "You may get up now but stay close to the property line all the way back to the trees," Charlie advised.

"Hey, by the way, where are you taking me," Annie finally asked.

"Thunder has escaped the hands of Jack and Lorenzo for now and is hiding in a spot that only he and I know about. I am taking you to him because he wants to see you before he is captured," Charlie explained.

Annie began rambling about coming face to face with Thunder. Forgetting her bravery a few hours earlier, she exclaimed, "I'm nervous, Charlie. What am I going to say. Let's see. How about—okay, Father—no, that is not the right approach. Oh, dear."

"Will you just shut up! You are making me lose my direction. We don't have much time," Charlie cautioned. He softened his caw and told Annie that she would have the right words when she saw Thunder.

"I smell a freshness," Annie told Charlie as she raised her head and sniffed the air.

"We are almost there. What you smell is the spring water. It's like a fresh breeze coming in off the ocean. It used to be a roaring gush, but now it is only a trickle," Charlie said as he inhaled so big he fell right off Annie's back.

"Oops," Annie laughed.

Annie heard Thunder bawling and knew they were very close. She took a deep breath to gain courage and bawled softly to let him know they were coming.

"Annie, it gets a little tricky now. You have to work your way through this maze of briars without getting stuck. Pay attention and don't be thinking about what you are going to say," Charlie said with that commanding voice once again.

"Ouch. Ouch. Ouch," Annie whined as she pushed her way through. "Charlieeee, I'm stuck," Annie blared.

"Oh, brother. You are not stuck. That is just a tiny, thin branch, and you are acting like it is a huge oak tree. Now move it!" Charlie squawked. Annie was just stalling because she was contemplating her speech to Thunder.

"Whew, we are here, Annie," Charlie said, exhausted from the challenge. "Thunder, can you hear me?" Charlie called quietly.

Annie crouched down as she heard a rustle coming out of the tunnel. She was shaking just a bit, but at the same time she began to relax. As Thunder appeared, he didn't seem so big after all.

The look on his face had softened, and he was gently approaching Annie and Charlie. "Hello, my dear Annie." Thunder called fatherly.

"Uh, hi, uh, Thunder, uh, Father," Annie reluctantly answered.

"Annie, listen carefully for a few moments, and then if you would like, you can talk when I finish," Thunder said with tenderness. "Cycles of life continue their circle. Titles are unimportant. Kings and queens of herds come and go. New leaders must come forth. Annie you are a leader, not an orphan. Your assignment was decided long before you were born. You have an inner strength and an outward demeanor that will help you not only to oversee the other cows but to take care of all the other animals as well. Esther is to be one of your mentors. Today, I realized that I must be moved to a new farm to begin another cycle of life. I am not unhappy about the decision Jack and Jan have made, but they also are given an assignment and must keep the cycle going. So, they have been given instruction to provide a seasoned bull for breeding purposes to a smaller farm. I have long outgrown being the "mighty king of the pasture" as I professed to be. There will be a younger bull sent here by the Cow Association to watch over all the heifers of J Bar J Ranch. This will be a good change and, I must say, a challenge with you in their face," Thunder said humorously. "Do you understand what I have said, Annie?" Thunder asked.

"I suppose," Annie muttered. "I believe that is why Mother talked to me so much before I was born. It was a school and training session. Although I didn't understand then, I am beginning to put some of the puzzle together now," Annie admitted. "I have such a love for the farm and all the animals that I want to help them, especially those who are alone and unloved." I will miss you, but know that your love and strength will always be with me." Annie spoke so lovingly.

"Annie, you are wise beyond your age and you have much understanding. Not everyone is chosen for such an assignment as this. You must remain humble and caring or risk losing the gift that is within you. As long as you remember this, you will be a valuable asset to the farm. And, yes, I will miss you too, but know that part of me will always be here. One day you will understand more. For now, let's hang on to the good things. Oh, yes, one more thing. Catacombs has something to tell all of you. Be sure to find out what he has been hiding," Thunder directed. "Now, I want to surprise Jack by not putting up a fight. Well, maybe I should kick and buck just a little," Thunder laughed.

"Thunder, I know you are in here somewhere. Come on out," Jack called. Thunder couldn't resist. He charged out of the brush just like he always did and took off bucking and jumping, with a big grin on his face. Jack was in pursuit as he threw the rope around Thunder's neck and had the grain bucket in his hand, bouncing right along. Thunder ran Jack ragged around and around the pasture.

Jack finally sat down, put his head in his hands, and said, "I give up." Then he felt a tug on the bucket and looked up in Thunder's face. He jumped up and knocked over the bucket, spilling what little grain was left all over the ground. He started to run but noticed Thunder began eating the grain. Jack picked up a big limb that was close by, just in case Thunder tried to pull any tricks, and moved cautiously toward him. Thunder was laughing heartily, pretending to enjoy the grain.

Annie and Charlie were hysterical as they stood by the tractor watching the whole thing.

"Hey, old boy. You gonna be good for me now?" Jack nervously said as he carefully put the rope around Thunder's neck.

"Uh huh," Thunder snickered.

Jan stood by the truck to assist Jack in loading Thunder, as Lorenzo was waiting to drive away.

Annie stood lifeless, watching the truck until it became a speck in the distance. Then the atmosphere became charged with electricity, and a ray of hope filled Annie as she could hear Thunder's voice ringing in her ear. "You have an assignment and are a leader, not an orphan." She stood majestically erect like a real Hereford, threw her head in the air, and swung her tail with passion. Annie had the strange sensation that she had just been splashed with a fresh new paint of bright color. J Bar J Ranch stood at attention, and the animals were in awe as they observed Annie's undaunted character. The buzz of the animal kingdom could be heard in every valley. Stinky, Mellie, and Mitzy scampered up and stood right by Annie's side with their tails loyally in the air.

"Let this day be one to remember. All of us have a job to do, and we must remain faithful. J Bar J Ranch is our home. Jack and Jan deserve our love. I will give care where needed and treat each of you the same regardless of your heritage. Now let's all go see what Catacombs has been hiding," Annie concluded.

CHAPTER EIGHT

Catacombs was stretching his flat head up over the bank to see what all the commotion in the pasture was about. He gasped so hard that he swallowed some of the pond water and became choked when he thought the humans were assaulting Thunder. "Stop. Please stop," Catacombs screamed. No one listened. "Don't you understand. Thunder is not such a bad guy," screamed Catacombs again. Still no one listened. Catacombs began swimming rapidly so he could forcefully propel himself into the air so someone might notice. Then, he could help Thunder. He catapulted himself at least twenty feet in the air and landed with a loud splash. Again, no one noticed. Frantically, Catacombs tried again. No one came. Catacombs became motionless, realizing there was nothing more he could do.

Catacombs was just about to dive to the bottom of the pond when he heard voices in the distance. "Someone is coming. The humans heard me and are going to help Thunder," Catacombs excitedly yelled. He quickly swam back in the direction of the bank by the oak tree so he could be ready to tell them that Thunder wasn't really as ornery as he acted. But, much to his surprise, when he reached the bank there was Annie and the rest of the farm animals.

"Catacombs, Thunder tells us you have a secret to reveal to all of us," Annie said getting right to the point.

"I am not obligated to tell you one thing. I want to know where the humans have taken Thunder," Catacombs demanded.

Annie didn't hesitate. She immediately told Catacombs, "Thunder has talked with me, and everything is alright. He has been transported to the auction barn so he can be sold to another farm for breeding purposes. I will explain all about it some other day. Now, Catacombs, what truth do you have to tell us?" Annie persisted.

Catacombs had forgotten all about his bargain with Thunder, and he began telling the biggest tale that had ever been told on J Bar J Ranch.

"Well, about twenty-five years ago my mammy and pappy lived in the Amazon River in South America. Part of the Amazon is in Brazil, and the rest is in Peru, Ecuador, and Bolivia for a total of about 3,900 miles. I was just a young lad and didn't like it there because of all the piranhas, pythons, and crocodiles. One day a canoe came my way, and I latched on to the bottom to set out for an adventure. During one of the drenching rains in April there was a severe flood that projected the canoe out into a tributary that would lead me to the vast ocean. I fought off sharks, eels, and enormous whales. Why, once, a dolphin even rescued me. He threw me up on his back and told me to hang on. His back was pretty slippery, but I locked myself in place and rode for miles. I eventually ended up in the Ohio River," Catacombs continued as his captive audience listened intently.

"I dodged every fishing worm that came my way during my journey. I certainly didn't want to get caught so someone could fillet me and put me in a skillet. One day I noticed a big fishing net full of all kinds of fish in it, and I swam over to investigate. That was a big mistake. I unwillingly ended up joining them. We were taken to the zoo where I had to fight off seals, polar bears, and those big, old, black vultures," Catacombs went on and on.

"I became real good friends with one of the zookeepers named Gungaden. I think he was from Africa. He was real nice and used to feed me extra fish food. But, as time went by the zoo was getting rather boring, and I asked Gungaden if he could find a more lively environment for me. He said he would try. The very next day Gungaden told me he had good news. One of his best friend's brother's uncle named Jack wanted to stock his pond with flat head catfish. And, my dear colleagues, that is how I got to J Bar J Ranch to become the monster of the deep," boasted Catacombs. "Yep, I am the one who has scared all the fisherman and all of you animals over the years," Catacombs arrogantly said. "I am the only phantom in this pond. There is no other," Catacombs bragged on and on. He told the story so well that he began to believe it.

Annie brought him back to reality when she said, "Catacombs, that is the most preposterous, bunch of poppycock I have ever heard Although I will have to give you credit, you almost had me believing because your story was so convincing." Annie laughed heartily.

From high atop a tree, Charlie launched off the limb and catapulted himself in a downward spiral, stopping just short of the water and landing on Catacombs flat head.

"Ah, Charlie, so happy you dropped in," Catacombs said sarcastically as he shook Charlie off his head.

"Hey, I was just coming to hear more of your adventure. Did you really ride on a dolphin's back through the ocean?" cawed Charlie longingly.

"Charlie, it was awesome. There were two dolphin's side by side and..."

Before he could finish another tale, Annie stopped him. "Catacombs, please. You know you didn't ride on a dolphin's back. Now quit fibbing to Charlie and the rest of us," Annie commanded.

"You are right, Annie. I was just dreaming and got a little carried away," Catacombs apologized.

Catacombs flapped his tail on the water and began saying, "Annie, Annie, Annie."

All the other animals chimed in. "Annie, Annie, Annie."

Charlie flapped his wings in tune. The leaves on the trees clapped their hands. Bah, bah came from the sheep in the meadow. Grunt, grunt went the hogs.

"Long live Queen Annie," Stinky cried.

"Meow, meow," sang Constant.

Francy cheered loudest of all. "Annie, your character is truly undaunted. Forgive me."

Esther, Bandit, and Arizona began circling Annie, crying "Three cheers for Annie." Their voices echoed throughout the valley.

Annie carried herself with a charisma that only she could do. Watching over all, she became loved and respected as she continued roaming the pasture each day.

CHAPTER NINE

The leaves were falling from the Oak trees, as if in slow motion, not wanting Fall to come too soon. Annie was restless as she scurried diagonally through the pasture, rather than taking her normal jaunt around the perimeter. Charlie was taunting the Blue-jays as they tried scavenging the left over grain. Mellie teased Mitzy because she smelled so bad. Stinky intervened. Catacombs was too old to do anything but float on his back and observe the cloudy sky. Arizona and Bandit were lying in the barren pasture sunning themselves wondering why Annie was so restless.

Sam barked loudly as the truck pulled up from Megiddo's Auction Barn. Now Annie realized why she was so restless. She recalled what Thunder told her about a new bull coming to J Bar J Ranch.

"This must be the day," Annie thought. At that moment the most beautiful gray bull Annie had ever laid her eyes on exited the truck. Not only was he beautiful, but his presence projected a commanding authority more powerful than Thunder. There was one definite difference—the countenance on his face was ever so soft, not disgruntled. Annie thought surely that he had come from Heaven. She could barely breath. It was love at first sight!

Jack broke the silence as he announced, "Meet Nubian, our new Brahman bull. He was shipped directly to J Bar J Ranch from southeastern Europe. Nubian will be used for breeding purposes. He may look fearsome, but I assure you he is tame and kind," Jack confirmed.

"Straight from Heaven," Annie sighed. "Europe must be close to Heaven to produce such a splendid animal," Annie repeated.

Nubian raised his head with confidence and sniffed the air that surrounded his new home. He truly was a magnificent animal. He weighed at least two thousand pounds and had a pronounced hump over his shoulders and neck, horns that curved up and back, and drooping ears. Gray was his predominate color, with a hint of deep, black shading on his fore and rear quarters.

Nubian bellowed a charming but commanding greeting to all the animals. He instinctively knew he would like J Bar J Ranch and wanted the animals to feel his strength and comfort.

The twinkle in Nubian's eye when he spotted Annie went unnoticed, except by Stinky. The enormous grin on Stinky's face brought Annie about-face. "You look as if you need a dentist. What is wrong with you?" Annie said between clenched teeth.

"Oh, nothing, nothing at all," Stinky giggled as she trotted off.

To avoid spoofing Nubian on his first trip to the pasture, Jack led him a different way to avoid the cattle crossing. Jack explained each section of the ranch as he and Nubian walked. Nubian enjoyed Jack's calming voice. It made him feel like a part of his new home.

"J Bar J Ranch has been in the family for one hundred years and has one thousand acres," Jack bragged. "Nubian, did you know that Indians once owned this land?" Jack asked just as if he expected Nubian to answer. "I can show you the spot by the spring where they used to have meetings with the Indian chief," Jack continued.

Nubian's attention was drawn away from Jack's conversation to a black snake crawling along the path. He became preoccupied with the slithering motion and silently wondered which direction it would go. Nubian watched carefully as the snake glided along the edge of the grassy field. Suddenly, the snake became motionless—ready to attack the unsuspecting field mouse. Nubian stared in disbelief at the size of the opened jaw of the snake as it enveloped the whole body of the mouse. Nubian continued observing the snake as it closed its mouth and slithered away to enjoy dinner. "Poor mouse," Nubian thought, as he turned his attention back to Jack.

Approaching the meeting place of the legendry Indian chief, Jack and Nubian both became entangled in the thick brush that had overtaken the opening to the spring. Jack reached in his back pocket to get his gloves so he could brush the limbs out of their way. Then, recognizing this spot that had also been the hideout for Thunder, Jack laughed real loud and smacked Nubian's backside as he began recounting the day when he tried to corral Thunder for the stockyard. Nubian turned his head sideways and looked strangely at Jack, but Jack continued jesting and talking.

"Hey, big guy. Up here. Don't be surprised by Jack's actions. He thinks we are humans." Charlie cawed bravely, as he sat perched on a limb comfortably out of reach of Nubian's horns.

Startled, Nubian jerked his head upward. Nubian quietly stared at Charlie. Charlie became uneasy and flew to another limb. Nubian's eyes followed Charlie, but he said nothing.

Charlie felt a shiver crawl down his back, all the way to his claws, shaking the limb he rested upon.

Nubian finally broke the silence, "What role do you play around here besides eating dead animals from the roadways?"

Charlie went on the defense at Nubian's offensive remark and replied, "I happen to be a courier to warn the animals of impending danger and other stuff, thank you!"

"I bet you are a courier alright—of gossip," Nubian snorted.

Charlie annoyed at the whole introduction to Nubian, flew away to find better company.

Jack cleared a path just big enough for him and Nubian to squeeze through to see the long forgotten meeting place of the Indian chief. "I can almost smell the smoke from the peace pipe; can't you Nubian?" Jack exaggerated.

"Oh, brother, this guy really does think I am human," mooed Nubian, as he licked Jack's hand in response.

"Time to trace our way back down the hill to the pasture, Nubian. It will be nightfall soon, and I want you to meet Annie before you go to your stall. We will come back another time to see if the Indian chief shows up," Jack jested.

"Annie?" sighed Nubian. He remembered Annie alright, spotting her immediately. She was the pretty little calf with the big brown eyes that revealed her undaunted character. "I felt those eyes watching me even before I saw Annie. She is just beautiful," Nubian sighed again.

The descent to the pasture was gradual but steep enough that Nubian could not see Annie hiding behind the stack of old fence that Jack had torn down a few days ago. Annie peeped through the fence sections and watched attentively—so attentively that she didn't hear Stinky approaching.

"Caught you," screeched Stinky, as he tiptoed up behind Annie. Annie nearly jumped to the top of the stacked fence.

"Stinky, you practically scared the birthmark off my leg. Now, shush. I am watching the most incredible sight I have ever seen in my life," Annie whispered.

Stinky raised up on her hind legs, but she couldn't see anything. She climbed to the top of the fence and caught a glimpse of Jack talking to Nubian as he led him down the hill. "Oh, Annie, I think I, uh, see stars. Oh, yes, I do," Stinky mused as she sprawled herself over a piece of broken fence, pretending she fainted from the beauty.

"Stinky, you obnoxious little rascal. Come down from there before they see you," Annie commanded, as she kept one eye on Nubian.

"Suc cow, suc cow," Jack called for Annie.

"Oh, the audacity. Jack, PLEASE, don't call me like that. Nubian will think I am just an ordinary cow," Annie pleaded!

Stinky's eyes widened as she nearly rolled off the fence pile, and she replied to Annie's comment, "Annie, I hate to break the news to you, but you are a cow."

"That is it! Stinky, you and I are through," Annie firmly said.

"Ah, Annie, I was just playing around. You know I think you are the best cow in the whole wide world," Stinky said as she rubbed against Annie's head.

Annie couldn't ignore her long time friend. "Okay. We can stay friends, for now. But, I told you to get down before they see you." Annie commanded.

Jack spotted Annie's big brown eyes peeping through the fence pile, but he didn't tell Nubian. Jack called again, only this time he called, "Annie, Annie, where are you? Nubian, sometimes Annie is a little cantankerous. Don't let those big browns fool you. She is quite a lady, but she can easily manipulate you if you don't stay on your toes," Jack implied as he nonchalantly led Nubian toward the fence pile.

"Jack, so nice of you to come. What are you doing here this time of day?" Annie lazily said, as she walked out from behind the fence pile stretching her legs, yawning, and batting those big, brown eyes. She pretended she had not heard Jack calling.

"I thought you may have been sleeping, Annie," Jack said as he went along with Annie's shenanigans. I want to personally introduce you to our newest resident. You probably didn't see him when he arrived," Jack facetiously commented. "Nubian, meet Annie, the prettiest little heifer around," Jack winked as he tugged at Annie's collar. Annie blushed and looked away so Nubian couldn't see how embarrassed she was.

Nubian, trying to muster a clever greeting, remained speechless and dry mouthed. Each breath he inhaled became short and raspy. His thoughts were rolling across his tongue and coming out his mouth in un-intelligible, broken syllables. Becoming so ruffled by Annie's beauty, he dropped his head and began pawing the dirt with his hoof to totally avoid conversation. "What is wrong with me? All of a sudden, I turned into a two thousand pound muskmelon!" Nubian whined to himself.

"Come on Nubian. Your first day has been pretty full, and you are as red as the caboose on a train. You must have eaten some bad grass today," Jack said as he led Nubian away.

Annie could hardly swallow for the big knot in her throat. Not moving a muscle, she watched Jack and Nubian for what seemed like hours, until they were out of sight.

Stinky finally kicked Annie gently to see if she had crystalized. Annie didn't even realize that Stinky was on the earth. As a matter of fact, she didn't even know there was an earth at that moment.

"Good golly, Annie. I think I had better call the veterinarian or maybe the cupid doctor," Stinky said a little irritated. "Your behavior is totally unacceptable right now!" Stinky mumbled, waddling away to tend to Mellie and Mitzy.

The dirt beneath Annie's feet felt like puffy, white clouds. She delicately danced on her tiptoes, humming, 'Oh, What a Starry Night.' And, the bell around her neck was tinkling the same tune as she made her way to the barn.

Stinky was not impressed with Annie's humming or that noisy bell, when she finally reached her stall. "Quiet! You will wake the girls!" Stinky demanded.

Annie still didn't hear Stinky. She lay quietly dreaming about 'You know who,' most of the night.

"Good night, Nubian. You will be able to see Annie again tomorrow," Jack instinctively called, placing the heavy metal latch in position on the barn door.

"Do you suppose Jack really knows my thoughts?" Nubian questioned, buckling his legs under him and laying his head on the soft bed of straw.

CHAPTER TEN

Brilliant, finger-like streaks of amber frolicked across the darkened sky as the sun began to peep over the horizon. Annie awoke from a restful sleep, stretched real big, and took plenty of time to lift herself to an upright position. Feeling unusually chipper, she began singing, "La, la, la, la" and chewing her breakfast at the same time. "Today is a wonderful day," Annie dramatically sang in a high-pitched note, arousing Stinky from a perfectly sound sleep.

Stinky, really trying to ignore Annie, covered her head with the tattered horse blanket and cupped it around her ears. Mellie and Mitzy burrowed further down into the straw, agitated with Annie's early cheerfulness.

"Oh, Stinky, time to rise and shine. Mellie, Mitzy, breakfast is waiting. Time to go to the pasture to see if anything is new," Annie sweetly called.

Stinky was not amused. "Annie it may be daylight in Australia, but not in America. It is even too early for Rosa to crow. Take your annoying singing and get out of here," Stinky gruffly remarked.

Mellie and Mitzy chimed in unison, "Yeah, Annie, go outside and la, la, la. Skunks sleep later than cows anyway."

"Too bad for you. Jan has a whole basket of fresh vegetables waiting for Ruthie and the other animals," Annie said as she raised her tail, spun around, and huffed off.

Mellie and Mitzy peeped out from under the straw at one another. "Do you suppose she is telling the truth or trying to trick us?" they questioned. Their mouth began to water as they thought about a freshly picked, big, orange, juicy carrot.

Stinky detected mutiny. "Mellie, Mitzy, you are so gullible. Don't even think about it. Annie is enticing you. Anyway, Jan doesn't even get up this early, much less pick vegetables in the dark. And just how do you think you would find this so-called basket in the dark? Now, go back to sleep!" Stinky said with finality.

Before leaving the barn, Annie rooted around by the wagon to try and find that old spray can Jan always used when the barn smelled bad. Annie thought it would be a dandy idea to spray some on herself, so she could smell like fresh lilacs too. Of course, the motive was to have Nubian notice.

"Hmm..., this must be the one," Annie said, studying the correct way to spray it. "Let's see. Jan always holds it up in the air, but I will use my back hoof and jump on the end so it will spray me all over," Annie decided.

"Hiss, hiss," went the can as Annie's back hoof touched the nozzle.

"Hooray, it's working. I feel the cool spray on my belly and leg,." Annie grinned.

Annie rolled the can toward her front hoof and sprayed one more time, covering her neck and front legs. Some of the falling mist covered her back too.

Annie raised her nose high in the air to sniff the fragrance, but she could smell only the musty straw.

"Maybe the last spray is the one that has the smell good stuff in it," Annie thought. She stepped on the can one more time. "Pop, pop, pop," went the can, sounding just like a round of ammunition going off. Part of the shattered can rolled toward Stinky's bed of straw. Annie shrieked and threw herself into a skid to reach the can before it conked Stinky. Her front hoof touched the can, but the rest of her was going so fast that she couldn't stop in time to avoid landing where Stinky was comfortably sleeping. Stinky flew about four feet in the air when Annie's weight hit her. Mellie and Mitzy tumbled separate ways upon impact. Annie, temporarily stunned herself, waited for Stinky to descend from the air.

Landing with a thud, face first on Annie's bony back, Stinky groaned in agony, holding her tiny little nose, which was mashed from the fall.

Mellie and Mitzy gathered themselves off the floor and shook until their fur smoothed itself back in place. Both of them were jesting and pointing at Annie. Shrill laughter from the two of them rang out so loud that Stinky forgot her nose ached. Mellie was so excited that she ran around in circles. Mitzy, peeping threw her paws, shrieked again. They couldn't stop guffawing long enough to explain their actions.

Stinky was becoming a little peeved...until she saw Annie. "What... what..." Stinky tried to ask but couldn't. She, too, was chuckling.

Finally, Stinky calmed down enough to ask, "Annie, what in the world have you been into? You are purple striped," Stinky squealed.

"Uh, uh, you are lying," Annie gulped.

"Here, look for yourself," Stinky snickered, holding up a piece of an old, broken mirror.

Annie's body shriveled up when she saw a streaked, purple face looking back at her in the mirror. Then, Annie promptly fainted.

"Annie, Annie, wake up," Stinky said, smacking Annie's purple face. "Quick, Mellie, bring me some water out of the bucket by the door," Stinky yelled.

Mellie hurried over to get the water. She found an old rag hanging from the pitchfork instead and dunked it in the water bucket. Dragging it with her teeth across the floor, she took it straight to Annie and plopped it right on her face.

Annie shuddered awake from the cold rag. "What happened?" Annie asked in a daze.

Mellie and Mitzy quietly snickered. Stinky objected to their behavior and asked them not to laugh, although her lips were quivering from trying to stifle her own laughter.

"Annie, uh, before you fainted, you were looking into a mirror. Do you remember?" Stinky stuttered.

Annie screamed, "Yes, I remember. Would you please tell me how I turned purple? There is no way I can let Nubian see me like this."

"I am not quite sure how you got purple, Annie. The only thing I want to know is how to get you un-purple," Stinky mused.

"Funny, Stinky, real funny," Annie stated sarcastically.

"Hey, Annie, some of the purple is coming off your face. I bet the wet rag helped," Stinky said, as she began wiping the wet rag down Annie's leg. "Yep, it is coming off, Annie," Stinky confirmed.

"Hurry, Stinky, wipe it all off. The sun is up and I need to get to the pasture," Annie continued pleading.

"Okay, Annie, all clean!" Stinky said. "Mitzy, take this rag and bury it out of sight," Stinky commanded.

CHAPTER ELEVEN

Nubian brushed wood chips from his sleepy eyes, rolled over, and fell back to sleep. He stirred once again annoyed when he felt more wood chips falling on him. The deafening noise above his head gave away the culprit—a ruddy-looking woodpecker penetrating the barn' siding in search of his morning meal.

Nubian inhaled, lifted his head upward, and exhaled with a force of a mighty rushing wind. The puff of wind nearly blew the woodpecker's feathers clean off his body, spinning him around the rafter and leaving only a claw hanging on.

"If you make one more peep, Woodpecker, I will really knock you off that rafter," Nubian belted out, and then he turned over one more time to try and get some sleep.

The woodpecker flapped his wings in a frenzy and fled from the barn immediately.

Brilliant sunlight beamed through the cracks of the barn, drawing shadows of dancing dew drops on Nubian's face. After much consternation, Nubian felt that he should meet the morning with some sense of appreciation, so he pulled himself to an upright position.

Nubian wandered around the unfamiliar territory, sniffing each area to determine who might have resided there before he came. Stopping at the water trough, he cautiously drank, keeping one eye on the door of the barn. He did not want anymore intrusions to deal with today.

With water still dripping from his chin, Nubian froze like a statue when he heard a very strange noise just a few feet away. He quietly turned his head toward the sound, slightly peering over the stall to see if someone was there. A shadow was lurking, but Nubian couldn't make it out.

Nubian smelled an unpleasant odor, as he crept closer to the shadow. Precisely at that moment a baby field mouse squealed and ran between Nubian's legs to safety. Startled, Nubian leaped high in the air and smacked his head against an old horse saddle hanging above him. The saddle came crashing down and landed on one of the humps on Nubian's back. In the meantime, another mouse scurried past. With the saddle still in place, Nubian edged inch by inch, closer to the smell.

The strange, chattering noise continued. Nubian was puzzled. He heard the sounds but saw nothing. He strained his neck to see over the railing, and was finally able to see what the commotion was.

"Yuk, yuk, yuk!" Nubian bellowed, as he spotted the same nasty old snake that he saw in the pasture, eating more of those innocent little mice. Some of the dead mice were laying near the snake hole; others scampered every which way to avoid the clutches of the big, black jaw.

"Why are you eating all those poor, little mice, you creepy crawler?" Nubian pitifully asked.

"For your information, big fellow, Jack put me in this barn to eat those poor, little, innocent, mice, so they wouldn't eat all of your poor, little grain," Mr. Snake firmly told Nubian. "Anyway, if I didn't do my job, Jack would get rid of me and just bring in another snake—maybe one not as nice as I am," Mr. Snake threatened.

"Well, it may be your job, but it still disgusts me. Next time, can you be more discreet and stay completely out of my sight, when you're eating those helpless, little creatures," asked Nubian.

Mr. Snake, unconcerned about Nubian's feelings, wriggled away without responding to Nubian's request.

"I have wasted most of the morning now. I must get to the pasture," Nubian said. Sauntering toward the door, Nubian forgot about the weathered, old saddle on his back. Pushing the door open with his nose, he stepped out into the bright sunlight.

CHAPTER TWELVE

Annie skipped happily toward the barn door. She turned and called to Stinky, "Are you coming?"

"Go ahead, we will be out in a little bit. I want to brush the girls first," Stinky called.

Annie lifted her front hoof to step over the rotten wood on the door casing, and then she leaped out into the brilliant sunlight. She squinted her eyes to see if Nubian was anywhere in sight. He wasn't. Annie continued tiptoeing quietly and slowly through the gate to avoid being too anxious.

Charlie was bored again. His favorite past-time was to pretend to be a 747 jet plane. Starting from the highest tree branch, he would fly upward to gain as much altitude as the capacity of his lungs could possibly handle. With great precision, Charlie calculated how much time he would have before reaching the pasture floor. Then, taking a deep breath of the thin air, he would tuck his feathers to his side and propel himself to begin the descent. Charlie would even simulate smoke and sound as he careened to earth.

Charlie focused on the tiny speck below as he spiraled downward. The air became easier to breath, and the speck grew larger and larger as he rapidly drew closer. Approaching his make-believe runway, he recognized the speck to be Annie and screeched to a halt mid-flight. "Jumping turtle doves, Annie, why are you lavender?" Charlie squawked, just as Nubian appeared on the other side of the gate.

Still mid-flight, Charlie let out another screaming squawk, "Dithering jaybird, now I guess you think you are a horse. Why are you wearing that broken down saddle, Nubian?"

For just a moment, Charlie thought he may have hit earth and died upon impact. Maybe he was in Heaven, where cows are lavender and bulls are really horses. Closing his eyes and shaking his head to be absolutely certain that he was still alive, he decided that it was just his equilibrium out of whack from spiraling downward with such speed.

With open eyes and a half sigh of relief, Charlie said, "No, I am not dead. I really do see a lavender Annie."

Annie looked at Nubian. Nubian looked back at Annie. Both were thoroughly embarrassed at the circumstances.

Stinky, Mellie, and Mitzy came rushing out of the barn when they heard Charlie squawking.

Stinky gasped! "Trouble on the horizon, girls. Annie will never forgive us for this one. When they had been in the unlit barn, it appeared all the purple was washed off. But the sunlight shows the paint had stained her coat, and now she is a very cool lavender."

Forgetting momentarily about her own problems, Annie studied Nubian. "Wonder why he has that old worn-out saddle on. Do you think Jack is going to sell rides on Nubian?" Annie asked herself.

Nubian curiously examined Annie. "Does this breed of cow turn lavender at a certain age?" wondered Nubian.

"Holy moly, Annie, are you sick? Should we call a cow doctor that specializes in purple animals or, do you want me to fly to the garden and get a rose to put in between your teeth so you can perform in the circus," Charlie harassed. He was still unsure how Annie got in this predicament.

Feigning an illness, Annie lied and whined, “Yes, that is it, Charlie, I am not feeling very well. I must have eaten some purple grain, and it turned me lavender. Maybe you should help me back to the barn.”

“Wait here, I will ask Nubian, the horse, to give me a ride. I will tell Jan to call the doctor for both of you,” Charlie said, as he winked at Stinky.

“NOOOOO, Charlie, you traitor, don’t you dare!” Annie begged. She tried to jump up and grab Charlie’s wing, but instead fell right into Nubian’s saddle, with both back legs dangling in the air.

“Why, Annie, if you wanted a ride, why didn’t you just ask,” Nubian kidded.

Totally discombobulated, Annie embarked on a ridiculous, phony act. Weakly sliding off the saddle to the ground, she began wailing pitifully. “I feel faint. Please, someone get the smelling salts,” Annie cried dramatically. Peeping out to see if Charlie and Nubian were buying the award-winning performance, she continued bellowing.

Nubian shook the saddle off to show Charlie he didn’t want to be a horse, and then he hurried over to Annie. “Annie, please don’t faint. Grab one of my humps, and I will help you to the water trough,” Nubian lovingly said as he wiped away the dirt around her purple mouth. “I like you whether you are purple or tan,” Nubian assured her.

“Really, Nubian?” Annie said, batting her eyes triumphantly.

“That is enough to make you regurgitate!” Charlie gagged.

“Ditto,” Stinky yelled.

Nubian and Annie were totally unaware of Charlie and Stinky’s snide remarks. It was quite apparent that the “love potion” had diverted their thoughts.

Annie giggled as Nubian playfully tugged at her ear. Nubian boyishly laughed when Annie rubbed her nose against his nose. Nubian placed his hoof under Annie, and with one manly swipe, he lifted her up from the ground. "Why, Nubian, my dear, you are so strong," Annie scrumptiously purred.

"I will not subject Mellie and Mitzy to this foolishness. Head to the barn girls," Stinky called, and without delay, they left.

Mellie and Mitzy dramatized Nubian and Annie's love scene all the way to the barn. "Beloved, Nubian, you are a smashingly, handsome horse. May I be your queen and ride away on your saddle?" Mellie chortled.

Mitzy jested, "Annie, dearest, purple is a stunning color for a queen. I will be your king and bounce you around on one hump every day."

"GIRLS, stop that!" Stinky commanded.

Annie confessed the whole truth about the purple paint story to Nubian, who led her to the water trough. Listening intently, Nubian stuck his hoof in the water and tenderly splashed her. After he did this several times, the lavender began to fade, and Annie was almost tan again. Nubian grabbed Jack's work rag from the side of the trough and rubbed Annie from top to bottom, explaining as he rubbed, "I don't want the evening air to chill you, Annie."

Standing back looking at Annie, Nubian kidded, "Hmm... purple was more colorful. Suppose we can find that paint can again, Annie?"

"If you are trying to be humorous, that would be NOT," Annie clowned.

"May I walk with you to the barn, Ms. Purple?" Nubian asked, bowing down.

"No, but you may give me a ride, Mr. Horse," Annie responded.

"Stinky, are you still awake?" Annie softly called, when she quietly entered the barn.

Stinky felt the sincerity in Annie's voice, but she didn't want to talk. She ignored Annie's call.

"Sleep tight, my best friend?" Annie said as she turned into her stall.

"Great, Annie. Now I really feel like a heel!" Stinky whispered to herself.

Not able to sleep, Stinky pushed herself carefully up over the straw so she wouldn't wake the girls. She waddled over to Annie's bed and shook Annie to awaken her. "Okay, Annie, tell me what is on your mind. Well, I know what is on your mind... just give me the juicy details," Stinky smirked, rolling her eyes.

"Stinky, don't be upset. You are still my best friend in the whole universe," Annie swore, by signifying the usual high five oath. "It is, it is... oh, I don't know quite how to explain it. I just, I just...LIKE NUBIAN VERY MUCH, Stinky. That is all! There, I finally got it out," Annie delightfully confessed.

Stinky relaxed her thoughts enough to realize that Annie was not deserting her or the girls. "Annie, I selfishly thought that you would not be you anymore and that you would not want my family around if you and Nubian liked each other. I know that is just plain tomfoolery! It only means that our family will get bigger and happier, right?" Stinky asked, looking for reassurance.

"Well, now let me think about this. That means that if I have a baby 'skunk' you will help care for it," Annie analyzed.

"Annie, for the tenth time! You will not have skunks; you will have cows," Stinky told her again.

"Oh, I forget sometimes. Anyway, we will all still remain family. I am sure about that," Annie promised Stinky.

"Good. I am going to bed now. Night Annie," Stinky said.

CHAPTER THIRTEEN

Annie was awakened by Charlie pecking the top of her nose. She jumped up so fast that Charlie went sailing and landed right on his beak.

"Oh, no, I am going to be the only beakless crow in the whole world," shrieked Charlie. Rubbing his beak with his wing, he realized no harm was done because he had landed in a pile of straw.

"What time is it, Charlie? Why are you here?" Annie asked sleepily.

"Nubian has been hurt pretty bad, Annie. He was out nosing around and had his sniffer where it didn't belong. You know, where that big hole is dug under the fence row over by the pond? Farmers have been trying to trap that rascal raccoon for decades. He has just been too clever. The only problem now is that Nubian has his foot caught in the jaws of the steel trap meant for the raccoon.

I was sound asleep, snuggled under my feathers, and perched on my favorite tree. I kept hearing this agonized cry, but I thought I was dreaming. The wind just kept blowing the sound of the cry in my direction, and that is when I shook myself awake. You could hear the bellowing clear across the field.

Not wanting to lose the direction of the cry, I walked carefully down the tree. I put my ear to the ground and could tell that I was to follow a direct line to the pond.

I took flight, but kept very low to the ground. What had been a loud cry now became a pitiful moan, as the distance between me and the cry got closer. I could see a large animal outlined by the light of the stars, and I realized immediately that it had to be Nubian," Charlie explained.

Charlie, still a little afraid of Nubian, kept a safe distance between them as he called, "Nubian, is that you? Are you okay?"

"No, I am not okay, nimble brain!" Nubian gruffly replied.

"Now, this sounds familiar—like Thunder used to. If I have to take this same abuse, I am not sure I want to help Nubian," Charlie said to himself.

"Charlie? Help me." Nubian cried.

"Oh, brother, here we go again. Another 2000 pound sniveling milksop," Charlie cawed.

"Nubian, just tell me one thing. Why is it that all of you big, bad bulls are such babies?" Charlie asked.

"How should I know, Charlie? Are you going to help me or not?" Nubian whined.

Charlie examined the area to see if there was something he could pry between the glaring teeth of the trap. "It is a little spooky looking around over here in the dark, Nubian. Shadows of fallen tree limbs look like big alligators lying in wait for a meaty, little crow to eat," Charlie confessed.

"Nubian, I think this big limb will work, but I am going to need help. Stay right here until I go get Annie," Charlie said, as he quickly took flight.

"What a dumb bird. Just where do you think I would go?" Nubian painfully groaned.

"That is the story, Annie. We need to hurry. I didn't want to tell Nubian, but his leg was bleeding pretty bad. Do you think Phyl could help us move that big tree limb?" Charlie asked.

"Good idea. Let's go get her!" Annie agreed.

Charlie hopped on Annie's back, and she ran as fast as possible to find Phyl.

"Phyl, Phyl, wake up, wake up. We have a problem, and we need your assistance now!"

"But, I don't want to wake up yet. It is too dark," Phyl whinnied. Then she nuzzled her ears down in the warm straw so she couldn't hear their pleas.

Charlie was airborne in a split second. He pushed his claws out to the limit and landed square on Phyl's rear flank.

"Ouch, ouch, you brute. You wounded me," Phyl neighed.

"I thought that may get your attention. Now, get your pretty, little self up out of your pretty, little bed and follow us," Charlie commanded.

Phyl bucked a little as she was getting up and asked, "Where are you taking me this time of night?"

"Nubian got himself caught in a raccoon trap. Neither of us is strong enough to free him. That is why we aroused you from sleeping," Charlie clarified.

"Oh. Why didn't you just tell me that earlier, instead of gouging me with those vicious claws?" Phyl indignantly snorted.

Constant had his four legs wrapped tightly around the stall fence right above where Phyl had been sleeping. His head, braced by the two large nails on either side of the rail moved up and down in perfect motion with each musical snore, until he was aroused by all the ruckus below. Falling to the ground, Constant landed upright on all four legs, just like a cat is supposed too, and meowed his disapproval at the disturbance. "Can't a fellow get any sleep around here? Why aren't you perched on a tree limb somewhere, Charlie? Annie why are you hanging out with Charlie this time of night? Phyl, I think you have some explaining to do!" Constant demanded.

"Constant, please show some respect. Annie and Charlie have come because Nubian has been hurt. They figured I was the smartest horse around, so I have agreed to help them," Phyl bragged.

Constant began recounting what he had seen earlier. "I was out doing my usual midnight run around the edge of the pond, and I remember watching Nubian engaged in a serious snoop. I crouched down behind a clump of bushes and smoothed my fur real close to my body to appear as part of the scenery. Closing my eyes to just a thin slit of an opening, so Nubian wouldn't be able to see me in the dark, I sat perfectly still waiting to see what he was expecting to find. He must have sniffed for ten minutes in one place, but he never did appear to find anything exciting. I got bored and snuck away from him in the opposite direction, heading back to the barn to get some rest before daybreak. You know, where I was when you all started making so much noise? Besides, I need to get back to sleep, so get going if Nubian needs help," Constant sleepily purred.

"Nubian, I am back, and I have brought some help. How are you doing?" Charlie asked.

Nubian didn't answer quick enough. The reason they couldn't hear him responding was because his voice was too faint. Charlie, Annie, and Phyl rushed over to where he lay, just sure they were going to find him dead. Their breath was visible in the cool night air, as they all breathed a sigh of relief when they heard his pitiful voice.

"My leg is in such pain, and I feel so terribly weak," Nubian faintly whispered.

"Hmm... you probably have lost a lot of blood. Hang in there, and we will work quickly to free you," Charlie assured him. "Annie, Phyl, see the big tree limb that looks like an alligator? Both of you push it near Nubian's leg.

All of us will guide the tree to pry open the jaws of the trap far enough for Nubian to pull his leg out. One, two, three, push! Careful, we do not want to cause more injury to Nubian's leg. Push again! One more time, and I think we will have it," Charlie grunted.

Nubian felt the tension releasing. He wiggled from side to side, and at the exact moment he yanked his leg free. The steel trap snapped the huge limb like a matchstick. The other half of the limb broke free, sending Annie and Phyl reeling to the very edge of the pond.

Charlie knew he had no time to waste. He couldn't worry about Phyl or Annie. He remembered seeing the small first aid kit inside the garage close to the barn. Telling no one, he set out to find it. Charlie returned on the scene holding the first aid kit with his beak, just as Annie and Phyl climbed back away from the water's edge. Nubian was lying dreadfully still.

"Annie, check Nubian's pulse. I will start working on a tourniquet to stop the bleeding. Phyl, you lie down next to Nubian to keep his body temperature warm," Charlie instructed.

Opening the kit, Charlie found a roll of gauze, one bottle of antiseptic, some scissors, a little bit of tape, and some antibiotic pills. Charlie had the stuff strewn all over the place so he could figure out what to use first to begin administering what little first aid he knew.

"Nubian's pulse is weak but steady. I will get some of the antibiotic into his mouth, and his saliva will melt it enough to swallow," Annie informed Charlie.

"Good, Annie. I think I can manage this gauze. His leg is punctured but won't need any stitches. He may just have to stay quiet and keep the weight off of it for a few days," Charlie observed.

"Nubian is getting warm again. He is beginning to stir," Phyl reported, but never moved from his side.

Charlie rubbed the antiseptic on the gauze and wrapped it around the wounded leg. Annie successfully got the antibiotic in Nubian's mouth and confidently prayed, "You sent Nubian to us from Heaven. Now, make him well. Amen."

Catacombs emerged from the bottom of the pond and reached for his new glasses so he could find his morning meal. What he found was not exactly breakfast. The sun barely peeping through the clouds disclosed Charlie, Annie, Phyl, and Nubian sound asleep in one pile beside the pond.

Squinting worse than usual, Catacombs looked again to make sure he saw what he thought he saw. "Yep, my eyesight is just fine, and that is what I see all right, four scoundrels lying lazily by my pond. But, what in tar-nation are they doing here?" Catacombs wondered. "HEY, YOU!" screamed Catacombs.

Annie was the first to awaken from the high-pitched yell. She looked around, trying to remember why she was there. First, she saw Charlie, Phyl, and Nubian piled together. Then, turning her head toward the pond, she saw this thing staring at her with four eyes just inches from her face. Annie leaped backward, landed on her buttocks, and kicked Nubian with all four of her sharp hooves. Nubian bolted upward, sending Charlie soaring like a rocket into Phyl's blond, puffy mane. Phyl screamed in pain from the sharp claws and fell into the water, dragging Catacombs nearly back to the bottom of the pond.

At the same time Annie got up and began dusting herself off, she saw hundreds of bubbles rising up on the pond. Bracing herself against the tree stump and putting her face barely in the water, she hollered, "CATACOMBS,

PHYL!" Her voice reverberated through the water like a canon going off as it echoed in their ears.

Surfacing, Catacombs sarcastically yelled, "I may not see very well, Annie, BUT I CAN HEAR OKAY! You didn't have to burst our eardrums. We were floating to the top just fine!"

"Oops, sorry," Annie giggled. She was happy to see they were both okay.

Charlie recovered enough from the fall to find that Nubian was doing quite well, without any limp whatsoever. Charlie also felt proud because he wasn't afraid of Nubian anymore.

Standing perfectly erect, Nubian filled his lungs to capacity with a breath of the fresh morning air. He gratefully acknowledged his three friends for saving his life. "I didn't know that J Bar J Ranch came equipped with such a fine team of doctors. Next time I will not be sniffing around after dark in unfamiliar territory."

"No, you have it all wrong, Nubian! What you meant to say is that you will not be sniffing around PERIOD. Right?" Annie joked.

"Ha, ha, little miss goody cow," Nubian retorted.

"Okay, let's break it up you two. I am hungry. See you later," Charlie cawed.

"Wait, Charlie. I especially want to thank you. I was such a rapscallion when we first met," Nubian apologized

"A rap... what?" Charlie quizzed. "Oh, never mind. I accept your apology. Now, the highway is waiting," Charlie cawed again as flew out of sight.

"Yeah, I am hungry too. In fact, I believe I was about to get breakfast when I was rudely interrupted," Catacombs reminded Phyl.

"Well, you don't have to be so unkind, Catacombs. I certainly didn't plan to spend my first waking hours at the bottom of your stinking, polluted pond! And, besides, I am starving too," Phyl shouted, trotting off to find a bucket of fresh oats.

"Thanks Phyl. If you ever need help let me know," Nubian called.

"Annie, would you walk to the salt block with me? I need to replenish some of the minerals I lost last night from bleeding so much. Bet you are hungry too, huh?" Nubian teased.

"I will walk with you, but I must hurry before Jan or Stinky realize my bed of straw is empty. Stinky doesn't miss much and will be searching for me soon. Bet I can beat you," Annie told Nubian, skipping ahead of him.

"You think you can beat me? It will never happen miss brown eyes. Remember, I don't have a limp. You will be sorry you challenged me, my dear," Nubian laughed, running so fast that he left a trail of dust behind for Annie to eat.

Annie coughed and then could see through the thin dust cloud. She immediately contemplated revenge and headed for the salt block.

"Nubian, Nubian, wait. You are going in the wrong direction to find the best salt block," Annie cleverly called out.

Nubian's bandage fell off when he stopped so suddenly. "Tell me which way, and I bet I can still beat you."

Annie charged in the direction of the foulest salt block on the farm.

Tyble, one of Jan's grandsons, was competing in a science fair at school and asked Jan if he could research chemical reactions from salt blocks when integrated with other ingredients. Jan agreed as long as he used safe products and kept a log of the tests.

First he mixed concoctions of household vinegar and milk to rub on a section of the salt block. When applied, the vinegar sizzled a puff of white smoke, then fizzled out, leaving a small crater in one side.

Secondly, he tried laundry detergent smoothly blended with shaving creme for another section. He cautiously swabbed this mixture on with a cotton ball. This formula not only left a blue tint but actually penetrated all the way to the bottom side of the rock, leaving a very nasty smell.

Fairly disappointed in the first two tries, Tyble decided his third and final test would consist of shampoo intermingled with cool whip. Upon contact, mounds of suds formed and erupted like mini volcanoes. The volcanoes continued for several minutes, oozing its chemical mixture down the sides of the salt block. Tyble was quite pleased with this experiment. As instructed, Tyble carefully recorded his findings and returned to the house to tell Jan. She suspected Tyble only wanted to experiment, and there may have never been a science fair at all.

Annie continued in the direction of the infamous salt block—with Nubian right behind.

"Guaranteed best mineral block just ahead," sneered Annie.

Nubian was closing in. Annie purposely stopped abruptly. Nubian screeched to a halt digging his hooves in the dirt to keep from crashing into her. Annie took off again. She hid behind the lone, round hay bale that stood beside the salt block. Saliva flowed from Nubian's mouth when he finally caught site of what he assumed was the best tasting salt block around.

His tongue beat the rest of his body to the salty mineral. He licked so fast, that his taste buds didn't react right away. Nubian never noticed his tongue was turning blue. The taste bud alarms ultimately went on the defense. Nubian's eyes bugged out, gag reflexes went on alert, odor pushed through his sense of smell, stomach churned, and his tail went into a spin.

Annie was laughing so hard she had to cross her legs to keep from using the bathroom all over the newly harvested hay.

Upchuck from Nubian's wide opened mouth spewed ten feet in every direction. His tongue was still blue, but the rest of his body had turned a drab green.

"Want some antacid, Nubian?" Annie tantalized.

"My stomach feels like it is on the outside. What is that salt block made out of—turpentine?" Nubian attempted to ask between gags.

"Nothing on the salt block can hurt you; it just tastes yucky. Come on, eat lots of this hay, drink plenty of water, and you will feel all better. I guarantee it," Annie assured him.

"Thanks, but no thanks, for your advice. I will find my own hay and water," Nubian firmly told Annie.

Nubian wanted a drink, but he had no intentions of drinking the water Annie suggested. He found fresh rain water in the trough closest to the pond. He drank so much you could hear the water gurgle in his stomach. Eating the hay that was close by did make his stomach feel better too. The green color also began to fade away as Nubian recovered from Annie's prank.

Annie's ears stood straight up in the air when she heard Stinky yelping her name. Calling her apology's quickly to

Nubian, she said, “Gotta go. I really do feel bad, but just couldn’t resist. I will make it up to you.”

“I accept your apology, even if you are a little scalawag. Besides, I need to be alone right now to get some rest before I go snooping around again tonight,” Nubian kidded.

CHAPTER FOURTEEN

Annie spotted Stinky coming out the front door of the barn, still calling her name. Annie lowered herself to the ground so she could scoot quickly under the big rut at the back entrance. Once inside, she hurried to her stall. Using her nose, Annie messed up the hay to make it look as if she had slept there. Sprawling her body the whole length of the stall, she casually shouted, "I am here, Stinky."

Stinky stopped abruptly and stood up on her hind legs to see if she could see Annie. "Annie are you out here?"

"No, Stinky, I am here in the barn," she called again.

"There is no way that Annie is in that barn. She has been up to no good I just know it," Stinky muttered to herself.

Stinky let herself back down on all four legs and proceeded back to the barn with a commanding authority. "Annie, you may think I am really dumb, but I know you quite well, missy, and you were not in this barn when I went outside to find you. Do you want to tell me where you have been all night, or do I have to spray my scent in your direction to have the truth come forth?" Stinky ordered, as she turned and raised her tail in the air toward Annie's face.

Annie jumped up, kicking and bucking. "Stinky, you primitive little mammal, don't you dare come near me with that thing," Annie screamed, running around the wagon.

Stinky grinned from ear to ear as she chased Annie, knowing that she had been de-scented long ago when Jan first found her. "I'm going to spray you real good, Annie," Stinky taunted, keeping her tail high in the air chasing after Annie.

Annie was running in circles around the wagon to escape Stinky. Out of breath and dizzy, Annie stopped for a moment and leaned against the wagon wheel. "Okay, Stinky, I give. Take your fluffy tail and move way over behind the ladder so I know for sure you aren't going to spray that thing, and we will talk," Annie huffed and puffed.

Stinky turned her tail and ran backward toward Annie as fast as she could go, giggling under her breath.

Annie shut her eyes, squealed, and climbed halfway up the wagon. She was sure this was it. Stinky was going to blast her. For that instant she felt doomed. "I will be ruined for the rest of my life—both smelly and purple," Annie dramatized. Actually, there was only a faint stain of purple remaining on her belly where no one could see it. Annie barely opened her eyes to see where Stinky's tail was pointed, but she couldn't see Stinky, who had moved out of sight to see what Annie would do next. Annie cautiously slid down the wagon. Looking from side to side, she stepped quietly toward her stall.

Stinky jumped out from behind the horse blanket and yelled, "BOO!"

Annie was so startled that the bristles on her back jumped higher than she did. "Stinky, now quit this game. I told you we would talk," Annie whined.

"I just had to have a little more fun, Annie. Okay, poor baby, you can start talking now," Stinky whined back.

"You scared my memory away, Stinky. Now, I forgot what you wanted to know," Annie joked.

"Of course you did, Annie. You will have to come up with a better excuse than that," Stinky challenged.

Annie began to relay the whole story of how Nubian's leg was caught in the trap meant for that rascal raccoon and how Charlie came into her stall to ask for her help in the wee hours of the night. Annie also explained why she hadn't asked for Stinky's help: they didn't want to awaken Mellie and Mitzy. Stinky was really surprised that they were able to convince Phyl to help them too, because she hates to be aroused from her beauty sleep.

Annie was still relaying parts of Nubian's rescue when she and Stinky heard the barn door creak. Annie ran to her stall, and Stinky scampered behind the horse blanket again.

"Annie, are you awake? I have come to tell you good news," Jan called.

Annie's insides did a flip. She remembered the last time Jan said she had good news—Thunder was to be taken away. Stinky peeped out from her hiding place to catch a glimpse of Annie when she heard what Jan said. Annie saw Stinky and looked sadly in her direction. Annie swallowed real hard and prepared for the worst, as she moved forward from her stall so Jan could see that she was there.

"Why, Annie, what is the sad face? This is a grand day in your life. You have graduated to the big, new barn that we began building before you were born. It is better equipped with 14' x 14' stalls, which allow plenty of room for you to move around when you give birth to a baby calf. There will be lots of space in the loft for me to sleep if you need my help at any time. Annie, I am sure you will love the wonderful sliding door that does not squeak when it is opened. The new barn is not heated, but it is constructed well enough to prevent the chilling winter winds from seeping through. Our animals will stay comfortably warm and not have to shiver all winter. And, there will be no holes in the roof to let droplets of rain fall on your head, or no sun peeping through the cracks drawing creepy shadows all about," Jan kidded.

"Oh, yes, one more thing—Jack added a bright red cupola to the new barn. A cupola is a small domed structure on the top of a roof, and is really more for appearance than anything else. Jack wanted to have the best looking barn around, so he had the contractor add a weathervane in the shape of a horse on the top of the cupola. Of all things, Jack also had a 'dog barn' built for Sam, complete with his own cupola and a weather vane in the shape of a dog on top. You will see how 'Sam' the weather vane spins around and around when a storm is brewing," Jan laughed.

Jan looked around and pointed out the possibilities of use for the barn that Annie lives in now. "We will use this barn for storage until we decide whether to tear it down or not."

"Can Stinky and the girls come to my new home too? If my stall is so big, they can stay with me," Annie pleaded.

Jan didn't answer Annie. She continued telling her the new barn was also near where Nubian lived. "You will be living with Esther, Francy, and the others, but you will not notice them because the barn is so big. Don't fret, Annie. I assure you it will be much more comfortable in the new barn. You have time to rest for a while, because I don't want to move you until this evening. See you in a few hours, Annie," Jan said, as she carefully pulled the door shut behind her.

Annie began her usual pacing and then hollered, "Stinky, I know you heard all that? Get out here. We are going for a walk before Jan comes back. I want to see this so-called new home I am supposed to get. If there isn't room for you, then I am not going!"

"I heard everything that Jan said. For your information, I have seen the new barn. It is quite nice, but I am not sure I want to live with all your cow mates," Stinky admitted.

Annie was a little more than perturbed at Stinky when she asked, "If you knew about this barn, why didn't you tell me?"

"Well, I knew there was a new barn, but I sure didn't know you were going to be transferred. That is why I never even mentioned it. The girls and I were out for our evening walk enjoying the sweet smell of the wild flowers—a real contrast to our odor—and accidentally discovered a huge, red building with that funny thing on top. You won't believe the 'dog barn' Jan was telling you about. It looks like a big barn that shrunk, and it is so realistic that Sam may begin to think he is a cow. I do know for sure that the new barn is quite a distance from here. If you are serious about seeing it before evening, I suggest you get started," Stinky said.

"Will you show me the way, please? I've just got to know what it looks like in case I want to tell Jan I am not interested in moving," Annie said assuredly.

"Follow me," Stinky told Annie.

Stinky and Annie went outside from the rear of the barn to avoid being seen. They began walking at a rapid pace to get to the new barn quickly. Stinky turned around to see if Annie was behind her, but she noticed that Annie had slowed down. She appeared to be very tired and Stinky was concerned but didn't let Annie know. "Annie, are you sightseeing or what? We really don't have much time to see the new barn and get back before Jan returns," Stinky reminded Annie.

"Golly, Stinky, I don't know why I am so tired. I must really be out of shape. Are we almost there?" Annie huffed.

"It is just over the hill ahead of us, Annie. You may be able to see the cup...cup..., whatever that thing is called, even before you see the barn," Stinky told her.

"You are too funny, Stinky. That thing is called a cupola, and I can already see it," Annie laughed.

"RASBERRIES!" Mellie and Mitzi screamed when they ran up behind Annie and Stinky.

"Why you little varmints! You are lucky I didn't kick your fuzzy butts," Annie yelled, jumping about two feet off the ground.

The girls let out a loud giggle, ran between Annie's legs and straight up the hill to the barn, and blurted out, "Bet you can't catch us."

Anne regained her strength from sheer determination and accepted the challenge. She raced the girls, leaving Stinky totally behind. Stinky outsmarted all of them because she knew a shortcut through the garden to the barn. Annie, Mellie, and Mitzi reached the top of the hill and fell like dominoes when they saw Stinky leaning against the barn door with a big carrot in her mouth. In unison, all three shrieked, "Who carried you up here?"

Stinky was too sly for them. She answered, "My angel."

"Sure, Stinky. We believe you," Annie said, rolling her eyes and snickering.

Then, Annie quickly got up and began to run again. She still wanted to be first to enter the new barn. Reaching the door, she gave Stinky a gentle shove sideways and pushed her way through the side entrance. Annie let out a loud gasp. She was totally unprepared for the humongous area inside that door.

Mellie and Mitzi pried the sliding door aside and let out a similar gasp. Stinky dropped the carrot and hurried in to see what all the excitement was about. She too gasped at the enormity.

Mellie and Mitzi curiously sniffed around, chasing each other into the biggest stall. The soft bead of straw was very inviting, so they jumped in head first. Playfully rolling and tumbling, both girls stood as tall as possible, then dove into the deepest section of the straw, sinking to the bottom out of sight. Annie and Stinky hurried over to find them but could only hear their laughter.

"Stinky, this stall is big enough for ten families—well, at least five," Annie exaggerated, with her mouth gaped open.

"That is for sure. There will be plenty of room for us and a baby calf," Stinky agreed.

"One, two, three, four, five, six, seven, eight, nine, ten," Annie counted, walking around to see the stalls where the other cows might live. "Jan was right. I won't even notice Esther or Francy. The stalls are pretty private. Each one has its own feeding trough, along with a place for drinking water. Wow, look at this Stinky. There is a door to the outside from each stall too," Annie pointed out.

"Annie, I think you have seen enough to make a decision whether to move or not. The choice is not yours anyway. Jan will decide for you. Speaking of Jan, we are barely going to have enough time to get back before she comes," Stinky reminded Annie again.

"Oh, no. I have one more thing to check on. Show me where Nubian lives," Annie told Stinky.

"I can only point you in the right direction. We absolutely don't have time to walk there. Of course, I guess our angels could carry us to save time," Stinky smirked.

Mellie and Mitzi pushed their way back to the top of the straw and scampered to the next stall to jump in again. Annie and Stinky just shook their heads when they saw them. They looked like two little bales of straw running around with just the white tips of their tail showing, sneezing and laughing as they ran.

"Girls, we must go. Come here so I can brush you off," Stinky called.

Mellie and Mitzi continued romping and begged, "Just one more time, Mother."

"MELLANTHA, AND MITZIGALIA!" Stinky called with force.

Mellie and Mitzi knew this was for real when Stinky used their full birth names. Both promptly bolted out of the stall and stood at attention by their mother's side.

Annie pushed the weight of her buttocks against the sliding door to get outside. She turned to call to Stinky and caught her hoof in the track of the door, leaving half of her body standing inside, and half outside. "Ouch! Help Stinky!" Annie cried.

Stinky had Mellie on her lap brushing the straw away from her eyes. She dumped Mellie to the ground to rush to Annie. "Oomph," Mellie grunted.

Stinky spotted a crowbar propped against one of the stalls and attempted to knock it down so she could push it toward Annie. It was too heavy. Stinky used the side door to see if there was anything outside she could use to help Annie. Stinky was so intently looking around for something she could use that she didn't see Nubian standing by Sam's 'dog barn.'

Nubian had been out patrolling the pasture most of the day. He stopped to admire the cupola on top of Sam's new house. Using his nose, Nubian twirled the weather vane around and around, but he grew dizzy watching. He decided to try some of the fresh grass growing near the new barn. Nubian stopped grazing and tilted his head to try and identify the unfamiliar noise he heard. The noise was Stinky rustling through the taller grass closer to the barn. "What are you looking for, and why are you all the way up here, Stinky?" Nubian asked.

Stinky looked toward the barn, and sure enough, there was Annie's back end sticking out. Trying to distract Nubian, she fibbed, "Uh, I am looking for moles invading the new ground and just decided to go out for a stroll, Nubian."

Nubian saw Stinky looking toward the barn. "Stinky, now I know you aren't way out here just taking a nice walk. Besides, I see half of Annie sticking out of the barn door, and I suppose she is in an odd predicament. Correct?" Nubian smiled and started walking toward the barn.

"Annie is going to faint again when she finds out that Nubian saw her like this," Stinky mumbled to herself.

"Why, Annie, I don't think I have ever seen a cow try to get out a barn door backward," Nubian teased, as he shoved the sliding door open wider.

"STINKY!" Annie bellowed and, sure enough, pretended to faint.

Nubian quickly pushed her against the door to keep her from falling, using his hoof to free her leg from the bent door track. "Annie, you are okay now," Nubian gently mooed.

"I am so embarrassed, Nubian. I promise I am not always this much trouble. Thanks again," Annie said, turning a bright red.

Stinky was becoming restless because it was getting late. "Annie, we must go. Jan will have a posse out looking for you if she comes and you are not there," Stinky nervously interrupted.

"Nubian, I must go for now. Jan said she would transfer me to the new barn tonight. Can you come by in the morning, and we can graze for breakfast together?" Annie humbly asked.

"I can think of nothing else that I would prefer to start my day with other than you, Annie. I will join you for breakfast," Nubian gallantly answered.

Stinky ran to get the girls out of the straw again and hurried down the hill. Annie wasn't far behind. You could hear her laughing at Mellie and Mitzi, who still resembled two bundles of straw bales in motion. Stinky couldn't afford to take time to clean them up. She knew the wind would blow away most of the fluffy straw by the time they arrived home.

Perfect timing! Annie, Stinky, Mellie, and Mitzi just cleared the rut into the back of the barn when they heard Jan unlatch the front door.

"Annie, I have decided to take you to the new barn in the truck. It is pretty far to walk this late. I will be back as soon as I load some of the extra ropes, shovels, and salt blocks," Jan explained.

"You don't have to explain the distance to the new barn to me. I just returned from there, and I am exhausted," Annie replied.

"Annie, the girls and I will wait until tomorrow to join you. I certainly don't want Jan to suspect anything, and besides we are too tired to make the trip tonight. It will be too crowded in the truck, and we couldn't hide," Stinky said as she and the girls snuggled under the badly tattered horse blanket.

Jan led Annie out to the truck and guided her safely into the back. Stinky was right—there was no extra space. Annie didn't have much room at all. Jan drove fast, spewing dust balls from the dirt road all around Annie. She sneezed, coughed, and sputtered as she was tossed from side to side because of the bumpy road. Finally, the truck came to a halt. Jan threw the gear into park, turned the key off, and jumped out to free Annie.

"Annie, sorry for the rough ride. We haven't had much time to work on the road, but we will soon. I know you will be very happy here. You are the first to move. I will bring the others in a couple of weeks," Jan said, patting Annie's head. Leading Annie to the sliding door, Jan pushed, but she couldn't get the door to open smoothly. She noticed the track was bent. "Wait here for a minute, Annie. Something is wrong with the door. Jack must have pushed the door the wrong way."

Jan went in through the side door and found the crowbar leaning against the wall. She carried it over to the track and began straightening the bent section. The heavy work boots she wore helped push the crowbar against the tough metal several times. It wasn't completely straight, but it would allow the door to move. "There, I finally fixed it for now," Jan said frustrated.

Jan opened the door as wide as it would go, brought Annie in, and showed her the new stall. Jan went back to the truck, leaving Annie to look around. She came back with a hammer, a small wooden sign, and a brand new horse blanket, which she pitched over the side railing.

Annie curiously watched Jan as she began to pound away on the cedar post. Jan stood back, but she wasn't satisfied, so she reached up to re-adjust the sign. Stepping back again to admire her work, she asked Annie what she thought. It was then that Annie realized the sign said, ANNIE AND COMPANY.

Annie stared for a moment and thankfully mooed, "My very own name, but what does COMPANY mean?"

Jan understood Annie's moo. Annie, one day soon you will have a baby calf. When this happens, we will change the word COMPANY to whatever name you choose. I burnt the name, ANNIE, on the sign permanently, but COMPANY is only temporarily sketched into the wood and can easily be replaced.

Precisely at that moment, Annie felt a flutter within her. Annie's emotions were like a yo-yo. First, she cried, then she laughed. Jan wasn't quite sure why Annie began crying, but she cried right along with her. She assumed Annie was happy with her new home. Jan patted Annie's head and hugged her tightly around the neck. Annie stepped across the threshold of her new home. Jan followed. Exhausted, they both welcomed the soft bed of straw and immediately sank down into it.

Looking up at the new roof, Jan told Annie, "When I was telling you about the barn, I did forget to mention the skylight. See the beautiful stars shining upon you to keep your pathway lit during the night. But, remember I did tell you there would be no holes for the rain droplets to sprinkle your head. Annie would you like for me to stay with you tonight so you won't be alone, just like I did the first night you were born?" Jan hugged Annie again. Annie nodded in agreement. Annie pulled the blanket down around them with her teeth and they fell asleep in the new stall.

CHAPTER FIFTEEN

Stinky, Mellie, and Mitzi gathered the old tattered horse blanket and drug it to the door of the barn. "Mother, this is kind of sad to leave the place where we were born," Mellie sighed.

"It will be okay. We want to be where Annie is to help her take care of her new calf one day. Come on, she will be waiting," Stinky said, turning one more time to say goodbye to the familiar surroundings.

Jan stretched, yawned, and rubbed her sore back. "Whew, Annie, I am not as tough as I used to be. Next time I think I will have to bring my own bed. I filled your trough, so you would have fresh grain this morning. Jack promised he would have my breakfast ready for me. I will leave the door open for you to go out and look around, but please don't wander too far until I can show you the electric fence line. Bye, for now," Jan called.

Stinky and the girls were just coming up the hill and could see Jan waving to Annie through all the dust as she drove away. "Annie, we had a family meeting last night and have decided that we want you to make room for us in your new stall. Besides, you are going to need help with your new calf soon, and who else would have more experience than I," Stinky asked.

Annie was taken by surprise. How did Stinky know? Last night was the first time she had felt life within her, not even Jan or Nubian knew. Annie was very puzzled and asked straight out, "Stinky, do you know that I am going to have a baby calf?"

"Yes, dear. I have suspected for several days. Yesterday confirmed it when we were walking fast to visit the new barn. Remember when you were so tired? That is one very definite sign of being pregnant. The baby takes lots of nutrients from the mother. Therefore, you must be sure you eat correctly to supply yourself with nourishment. I will help you," Stinky motherly explained.

"When should I tell Jan and Nubian?" Annie sheepishly asked.

"I am sure they already know, Annie. It is hard to hide that extra sparkle you have. Your coat is so shiny, and your eyes have that extra pinch of love in them—for something special about to happen. I was explaining to Mellie and Mitzi how you would need our help soon. They weren't paying attention, but they will understand in a few months."

"You are right, Stinky. I wasn't sure why I felt so different. Now I am beginning to understand. There is really a new life developing inside of me. It seems so long ago that I was doing the same thing inside my mother. I had so much fun. I wonder if I will have a heifer or bull? Maybe I will name it after my mother, Maggie," Annie reminisced.

"I do know one thing for sure. I will not have a baby skunk!" Annie positively said.

ABOUT THE AUTHOR

Rosemary McCutcheon is a native of Indiana. She is certified through the Institute of Children's Literature, and is published through *Faith & Stuff Children's Magazine*.

She balances her hobby of writing, with dual positions as a Program Assistant at a National Church Headquarters, and the ministry in her local church.

www.ingramcontent.com/pod-product-compliance
Ingram Content Group UK Ltd.
Pitfield, Milton Keynes, MK11 3LW, UK
UKHW040017200726
13854UKWH00001B/247

9 780759 661240